CHICK-A-BOOM
★
FINANCIAL FITNESS FOR WOMEN

PATRICIA MARKS

Stoddart

Published in 1999 by Stoddart Publishing Co. Limited
34 Lesmill Road, Toronto, Canada M3B 2T6

Distributed by:
General Distribution Services Ltd.
325 Humber College Boulevard, Toronto, Ontario M9W 7C3
Tel. (416) 213-1919   Fax (416) 213-1917
Email customer.service@ccmailgw.genpub.com

03 02 01 00 99   1 2 3 4 5

Canadian Cataloguing in Publication Data

Marks, Patricia
Chick-a-boom: financial fitness for women

ISBN 0-7737-6060-1

1. Women — Finance, Personal. 2. Investments.
3. Portfolio management. I. Title.

HG179.M375 1999   332.024'042   C99-931457-2

Cover Design: Bill Douglas @ The Bang
Text Design: Tannice Goddard

THE CANADA COUNCIL | LE CONSEIL DES ARTS
FOR THE ARTS | DU CANADA
SINCE 1957 | DEPUIS 1957

We acknowledge for their financial support of our publishing program the Canada Council, the Ontario Arts Council, and the Government of Canada through the Book Publishing Industry Development Program (BPIDP).

Printed and bound in Canada

To You Who, Sniggy, and Alan
because I love you

CONTENTS

ACKNOWLEDGEMENTS

Chick-A-Boom exists because I came to believe that my unexpectedly interlinked experiences with fitness and finance, and the lessons I learned from them, had value for other women as well. But once the idea of this book started to grow, so too did the list of people whom I would now like to thank: Sabine Steinbrecher and her fantastic group at VORG for their enthusiastic confidence in both me and my book; everyone at Stoddart Publishing, especially Stephen Quick, Sue Sumeraj, and Kerry Breeze for always taking the time to listen to me and to answer my questions; Blair Drummie for legal guidance; and Gretchen Drummie for providing a writer's view.

A special thank you goes out to my Muskoka friends. Your belief in me and this book is of tremendous value to me.

Finally, I would like to thank the clients who became my friends, and the friends who became my clients.

INTRODUCTION

I could write a long drawn-out book explaining the virtues of investing and the value of financial planning. The first umpteen chapters could outline, define, and educate the reader to the investment world and terminology in a concise, scientific format. Or I could translate the entire financial world into "chick-speak" so as to take the fear and mystery out of it, but fail to explain the science of investing. Either way, by the time you reached the end of the first paragraph, you would be sporting that glazed-eye look that normally accompanies financial books, especially those directed at women.

Instead, what I propose to do with this book is help you to develop the solid financial basics needed to become financially fit, and make it an enjoyable process. Financial Fitness for Women is a vehicle that delivers the investing necessities and know-how needed to develop a healthy, wealthy, well-diversified portfolio and a keen appreciation of the market. Quite simply, it is a workout for your money and investment goals. I firmly believe that the reason so few women partake in the investment world is that they have had very little exposure to it. How can you participate in an active market, use all of its available instruments to get your money working harder for you, and reach your investment goals if you don't understand any of it? A girl's got to have a solid educated grasp of the market in order to make it work for her.

Financial Fitness for Women delivers this information through a metaphoric message likening investing to a physical fitness workout. I know from my teaching experience that women understand the dedication to a fitness regime and the results that come from that dedication. Not only do women understand what it takes, they've become fanatical junkies working towards the endorphin high. But female interest and participation in fitness is a relatively new social phenomenon. The health club was not always a female domain; it took both education and familiarization for women to feel comfortable there. All women need is for that same combination to be transferred over to the investment world, and financial fitness will result! In the same way that we managed to infiltrate the meatheads' control over the weight room, we can conquer the trading floor.

When you join a health club or begin a fitness regime you have motivation and a goal. The desired outcome is to attain a perfect physical condition. Everyone has a different view of perfection, but the general consensus from what I've seen and heard demands tight abs, a hard butt, shapely legs, arms that stop waving when you do, and the cardiovascular level of a marathon runner. These goals are not achieved through procrastination and lackadaisical interest, but rather through a serious focus blended with a fun factor. The basic components of a workout are the following:

- Stretch
- Warm-Up
- Cardio
- Strengthening
- Abdominals
- Cool-Down

Financial Fitness for Women also has specific components to be followed in order to achieve maximum results. Again, definitions of wealth and success vary from person to person, but for the purpose of *Chick-A-Boom*, the definition of financial fitness is not a specific dollar amount. Rather, the financial fitness workout is focused on the achievement of financial independence and self-confidence. Women are hit hardest with retirement shortfalls yet live the longest, and without enough money. Women are also prone to crisis investing, which means that only after a crisis (e.g., divorce, downsizing, or a death in the family), do they think about financial matters. By developing and following the financial fitness workout, independence, financial security, self-reliance, and confidence will ripple through female society like a 6-pack stomach — *guaranteed*! The basic components of the financial fitness workout, as shown with their synonymous physical fitness components, are as follows:

- Stretch: Mental Stretch to Recognize Female Strength
- Warm-Up: Warming Up to the Idea That a Woman's Place Is in the Market
- Cardio: Chick Picks, Cardio Blips, and Market Activity
- Strengthening: Cross-Training Investment Products — Time Is Muscle

- Abdominals: Retirement Planning Takes a Strong Stomach
- Cool-Down: Cool Your Risk Aversion with Comprehensive Confidence

This workout will help you develop investing knowledge that will aid you in your quest for financial independence. Have you ever fought to drag yourself to the gym and at the end of the workout felt energized and rejuvenated? The same sense of accomplishment can be achieved with your financial goals and can give the same release of stress. The main reason for women's lack of participation in the investment world is a lack of exposure to the environment. All that is needed is some information, education, and experience. Once the basics are provided, financial fitness will become a part of your life, like brushing your teeth or doing your nails. *Chick-A-Boom* will provide a clear introductory explanation of the financial world and help you become familiar with the terms and operations.

Have you ever noticed how frightening something can be if you have no previous exposure to that subject? You can feel quite ridiculous in all parts of your life at that particular moment, never mind how brilliant you may usually be in any of them. Self-confidence and success go hand in hand, and as your investments grow and maximize their performance, so do your self-reliance and strength.

Financial Fitness for Women will erase the stereotypical reputation that women have in the financial community as risk-averse ninnies who do not even know how to balance a chequebook. The reality is that women represent 45% of the workforce, earn a ton of dough, and with the correct tools can master the market and subsequently their money. Another outdated stereotype is that most women avoid the use of weights to increase muscle definition and predominantly stay out of the weight rooms of gyms. Weights are now a huge part of everyone's workout routine simply because of basic education in kinetics. Learning which weight exercises worked what muscle groups and how they increased energy consumption and metabolism rates provided women with the confidence and desire to incorporate this new concept into their workout routine.

Have you updated your financial fitness routine lately? Or are you still wearing leg warmers and rolling pennies? Have you developed a routine that reflects adequate savings and objectives to ensure short-term goals? Do you know how much money you will need for a comfortable retirement? Do you realize that you are missing the boat on compounding interest with each moment of investment procrastination? When you review your portfolio, do you feel the endorphins of financial security coursing through your veins? Or is the only time you start to sweat when you think about your finances?

Health and wealth are two of the most important components of any person's life, regardless of gender or age. There is health in investing — for example, stress and dependency are reduced. And of course maintaining a healthy lifestyle is an incredible investment. Unfortunately, women have been slow to recognize the powerful combination of health and wealth. The changes in the roles of women have created the need for a focus on women's financial advancement. There is a reason that Barbie no longer says, "Math is hard." Women are taking more control of their lives, and investing should be a huge part of that. Professional and social advancements make female financial fitness necessary. The days of women frantically handing their money over to the nearest shoe store instead of investing it are over! By following the financial fitness workout, you will experience an empowering state of financial strength and independence.

To all of you who think you are currently in a situation that is too far away from successful investing, I say "Bull!" (which, ironically enough, is your first introduction to investment terminology — a Bull Market is a rising market, and the opposite is a Bear Market). I myself went from investment void to investment adviser, and it was just a question of education — simply training myself in a previously unknown field. From a state of *cannot* to *can*, I changed my mindset to include money and financial goals. This is where the concept of Financial Fitness for Women was formed. I was working full-time within the investment industry, teaching aerobics, competing in triathlons, and even attempting to maintain all things social in my spare time. I decided that my professional and personal passions — health and wealth — despite seeming a strange combination, could be linked in a manner that would help define the mysteries of the financial world to women.

Looking at financial investing through the terminology and metaphors of physical fitness is something everyone can relate to, no matter what your age or level of fitness. It is all about setting goals and accomplishing them, just as when you join a health club or make a commitment to running or exercising. Goals — it isn't until you begin pursuing them that you realize how attainable they really are.

1

STRETCH

Mental Stretch to Recognize Female Strength

Once you have fought off the demons of the day and successfully arrived at the health club for your workout, the first step is to provide your body with a good stretch. The purpose of the stretch is to relax the body, focus on your breathing, and warm up your muscles so that you can and will respond to the level of challenge provided by your workout. The first step of the financial fitness workout, the mental stretch, addresses women's psychological differences. This is a mental stretch that will condition you to accept your intellectual and investment capabilities. It gives practice in building up confidence that will provide the acceleration you need for success in financial territory previously uncharted by women.

There is an absolute need for women to recognize their own self-worth, not only their capabilities in the investment world but in all of their worlds. Ideally, this recognition of self-worth will encourage a supportive relationship to develop between women. We might assume that there is a solid support system in place to combat the male dominance in society, yet ironically competition between women is usually much more fierce than between men. Women view each other as seriously threatening competitors both in private and professional relations. This attitude needs to be corrected so that women can appreciate each other's accomplishments and achievements without jealousy and insecurity tainting the relationships.

The first step is to get rid of the look — and you know what look I mean: that undeniable up-and-down motion we use to scan each other every time we meet. It is like watching two cats circle each other, eyeing the competition with acid-like warmth. The introduction could be in a professional or personal situation, but the reaction is always the same. Developing a more appropriate style of interaction would create a new strength for women. It would replace insecurity with common respect and pride in what our gender has accomplished. It would probably result in a new form of empowerment and drive. At the very least it would encourage a development of respect, both between and towards women.

Successful professional women should stop apologizing for being female. There is no need to dress down femininity, brains, aggressiveness, desire, and accomplishment. Think about what men would do if they had all of that to offer! Women should shout from the top of the skyscrapers, loudly and proudly. The shock of the social redefinition of women should have worn off by now, considering that it has been a while since the eighteenth century. Most professional careers are attainable by both men and women, and both genders are represented in most careers. Universities are pumping out male and female graduates in many fields with various degrees, and all compete for the same jobs. No longer can industries restrict female access because they are not part of the boys' club (although to think that the boys' club no longer exists is a serious mistake). The differences that society relied on to define gender roles have been erased. This is not to suggest that the roles of housewife and mother have been replaced by a role in the business world, but that more often than not, these roles have been combined into one.

Take a moment and consider all the demands on your schedule every single day, and think about how easy it seems to accomplish all that is expected of you. Congratulations. Every single day of your life is a miracle in multi-tasking, and you should be proud. Unfortunately, these accomplishments have not resulted in women's economic empowerment in the investment world. Salaries are increasing, degrees and training deliver professional careers that are juggled with family responsibilities, and any free time is divided between various social activities and health club workouts (you didn't think I was going to omit the gym, did you?). There is arguably very little time to dedicate to financial planning, but it is a need that should be addressed, and the sooner the better.

It's surprising that women aren't more confident and curious about entering the world of investing, considering their natural tendencies and patterned behaviour. By nature we are a more patient gender and are more thorough in our approach to decision making. Women perceive the long-term effects inherent in every situation and decision. As a rule, women read between the lines of everything because we want to be prepared for every possible outcome. This behaviour is developed in our archetypal psyches. As the sex that reproduces, lives longer, is predominantly in the care-giving role, and is usually the long-term planner, we do not make rash decisions without weighing all the ramifications. Women have displayed a rational and calculating manner in their development throughout history, and it can definitely be argued that in the role of investor a woman possesses the necessary ingredients for financial greatness and success.

The Patient Chick and Successful Investing

A successful investor needs to appreciate that a long-term buy-and-hold strategy will outperform the day-trading cowboys, hands down. When purchasing an investment product, shop around for the highest quality, best price, and best performance available. The more patient you are and the more rational your behaviour, the stronger the likelihood you will profit from your characteristics. The investment market is a creature unto itself, with seemingly inexplicable movements up and down. The reasons behind a stock skyrocketing in price or plummeting to the depths of a penny stock cannot always be linked to a specific news item or company earnings. Sometimes a company's stock price will just react to market influence and the investor is not able to find a reason.

The benefit of being an investing Chick is that we are patient. Therefore, if the price of a stock tumbles and other investors abandon ship, selling out despite taking a huge loss, the investing Chick will recognize the opportunity to patiently sit and wait out the storm. She may even see an opportunity to purchase more of the same stock at a cheaper price. (This practice is known as lowering your average cost. As a quick analogy, imagine that a fitness club is offering you a renewal membership at the same price as your original membership, but with three extra free months included. In effect, you would be lowering the average cost you paid on a monthly basis to be a member of the facility, buying 15 months' membership for the cost of 12 months.) Similarly, if the price of a stock jumped considerably, you can be certain some investors would be selling their holdings to take some of the profits. But the patient Chick would be likely to perceive that potentially higher gains might be made if she were to just sit still, enjoy the gains in her portfolio's balance, and wait for a possibly more significant gain.

THE BIG STRETCH: RISK AND REWARD

When you set out to increase your fitness level and physical strength, you create a fitness regime outlining your goals and a time frame within which you choose to work. With a structured guideline, you can identify your achievements and your shortcomings and therefore continuously challenge yourself in your quest for fitness perfection!

In order to successfully achieve your short- and long-term financial goals, you need to understand your risk tolerance and your objectives. You will need to create an investment policy that will identify your risk tolerance, your return requirements, and any constraints you may have.

Risky Business

Stretching before a workout is imperative to avoid injury and to loosen up your body in preparation for exercise. If you don't stretch, you limit the performance potential of your workout.

Risk tolerance is to investing what stretching is to your muscles. Risk tolerance is quite possibly the most important factor involved in investing. If you are not comfortable with the possibility of losses, your portfolio should be strictly made up of government bonds. There is very little risk involved in this type of investment, so the likelihood of loss is quite small — but so is the growth potential. There's a correlation between risk and reward when it comes to investing. The most risky arena is the stock market, but it also offers the greatest potential for gains. You can lessen your risk factor in the stock market by such methods as investing strictly in blue chip equities.

Blue chip companies are the icons of free enterprise, the names that created and to a large degree sustain the capital markets. Blue chip companies can be very easily identified as they make up the Dow Jones Industrial and the Toronto Stock Exchange indexes. IBM, General Motors, all of the charter one Canadian banks, Procter & Gamble, and General Electric are just some examples. By adhering to a strict policy of investing in blue chip companies, your risk level is lowered considerably. But whether you invest strictly in bonds or strictly in penny stocks, your risk tolerance level needs to be ascertained from the outset, so that you have something to measure your investment decisions against.

The best way to define your risk tolerance is to know what you are prepared to lose. The prospect of losing money is rather frightening, no matter how much you may have. But successful investing requires a level of confidence that acknowledges that your choices could result in a loss. If you are not at all comfortable with this possibility, you will not be comfortable with stock or any other risk-associated holdings in your portfolio. You will not be able to stomach the volatility associated with the daily movements of the market. The stock market is a cyclical animal that veers towards consumer products one day and turns to resources the next. If you are watching your holdings on a daily basis because your risk tolerance is so low that any loss is completely unacceptable, the only thing you will gain is an ulcer. This is not to say that loss is a guaranteed result of market participation; in fact, with a well-structured portfolio handled by a capable financial adviser, loss should be successfully avoided in the long term — but your route to the long term can have its ups and downs.

To further develop understanding of your risk tolerance, you need to know what represents an acceptable return on your investment portfolio. If long-term investing delivers higher returns on a consistent basis when compared to short-term market timing, you need to identify what are acceptable returns on a one-, three-, five- and ten-year basis. Once again, when you have established the guidelines and levels of risk that are acceptable to you, the likelihood of developing the confidence necessary to successfully participate in the market increases.

Risk tolerance does not need to be a permanently defined property — in fact, it is quite flexible and can change with the circumstances of the individual investor. Obviously, if you have a very small amount of money available for investing, your risk tolerance is going to be considerably lower. However, as your investment capital increases, you will be in a better position to increase your level of risk tolerance.

Age also comes into play when defining an acceptable level of risk. An industry rule of thumb is that the younger the investor, the higher the level of risk that is acceptable. This is basic common sense when you think about it. If you are two months away from retirement, the last thing you would want to do is increase your risk tolerance and shift your entire portfolio into one particular stock. At this point in your life, you would need to reduce your risk and increase your guaranteed investments to ensure that you do not live longer than your money lasts.

On the other end of the spectrum, as a 20-something just entering the working world with no mortgage payments, family responsibilities, education costs, or other such expenses, you are in an ideal position to increase the risk level associated with your investment portfolio. If you were to sustain a loss of capital, you would have a great deal of time ahead of you to make up the loss The quality of your retirement years is not in jeopardy. This chart outlines the correlation between investing and age:

LIFE CYCLE INVESTING

Life Cycle	Major Concerns	Risk Tolerance (% of Portfolio Invested in Equities)
Expense Years (20–35 years old)	Liquidity & Growth	40%+
Growth Years (35–55 years old)	Growth & Taxes	~40%
Balanced Years (55–65 years old)	Taxes & Security	~30–40%
Security Years (65 plus)	Safety & Income	~20–35%

As the chart illustrates, risk tolerance level is higher in the Expense and Growth years because the investor is younger and therefore more capable of absorbing loss. What this means specifically is that there is more time available to make up the loss with various other investments. A young investor has enough time to enjoy growth in assets because of the benefits of compounding interest. If your assets are increasing in value as a result of a rise in a stock price, and you don't plan on withdrawing the money from your portfolio, the value will continue to increase because of the interest earned.

When you are nearing your retirement years, the holdings in your portfolio are allocated to specific purposes, and therefore the room for risk is limited. These specific purposes could be the need for a retirement home, planning for medical expenses, travel and recreation, and money to live on; you will probably have set up your estate as well and will want to leave some money to your loved ones. Not exactly the time to throw it all into an Internet stock that looks like it could really take off!

In your 20s and 30s, high-impact aerobics and kick-boxing classes probably seem like a logical option for a workout. Nearing your 60s and 70s, a brisk walk and a yoga class might be a better program choice.

Many Happy Returns!

Return requirements are equally important to establish once your risk tolerance has been identified. Return requirements are what you need out of your investment portfolio — in other words, your portfolio's purpose. Have you initiated your financial plan to achieve a specific short-term goal, such as the purchase of a house, car, or cottage? Or does your new-found participation in the investment world represent a two-fold purpose such as a new car in the short term and a fabulously decadent retirement in the long term?

You must answer these questions in great detail in order to outline your ideal investment portfolio. The money that you put into your investment portfolio needs to be categorized. If you do not need the money in the near future and would like to put it towards your retirement savings, open up an RRSP (Registered Retirement Savings Plan) account so as to increase the performance of your money through a tax shelter (see Chapter 4). This return requirement — that is, investing for retirement — is called long-term capital growth. If, however, you would like to use your money for investing but would also like to maintain the liquidity for unknown future uses, an investment account would probably suit your needs better. Such a return requirement is best described as short-term capital growth with an emphasis on liquidity.

By correctly identifying your return requirements, you can increase the appropriateness of each investment choice you make. For instance, if you have chosen short-term capital growth with an emphasis on liquidity because you think that in three years' time you would like to purchase a house, locking yourself into a five-year deferred-sales-charge mutual fund would not be an appropriate investment choice. It would be better to choose an instrument that offers potential growth while at the same time is completely liquid, such as stock. Similarly, if you don't need your money from your RRSP for the next 20 years, investing in a long-term corporate bond that matures in 12 years and offers a 10% return would be an appropriate investment instrument.

In addition to income and liquidity, you also need to identify what type of return is more important to you: nominal or real return. Nominal returns are the numbers that show on your statement every month — the dollar value of your investments, as they exist in your portfolio. You get real returns when you take the profit you have made after purchasing an investment, sell it, and request that your financial consultant cut a cheque for you for the amount made. Nominal returns stay in your account and can be used for additional investment purchases, whereas real returns are taken out of your account and used elsewhere.

When you outline your return requirements, you might also wish to consider the currency you invest with. You may decide to open up an American dollar investment account, to participate in the strength of the U.S. dollar. In the same way that incorporating new moves such as Pilates into your stretching increases your flexibility and physical potential, increasing the diversity of your investment portfolio enhances your potential performance. As long as you don't spread your assets too thin, the variety could deliver greater returns. Learning to measure what is too thin is the key to success. If your assets are limited, you would not benefit from a U.S. account. When you and your financial adviser establish an investment policy, you will also establish appropriate asset levels that, once achieved, will lead to increased diversification, such as opening an American account.

The benefit of a U.S. account is that the U.S. dollar is much stronger than the Canadian dollar, as the Canadian dollar's value is reflective of much higher unemployment and welfare rates. The U.S. dollar represents a stronger efficiency as U.S. markets are made up of the most successful corporations in the world economy. The historic performance of the U.S. market indexes is statistically much higher than that of the Canadian market indexes, so that market is very attractive for investors.

A Bit of Caution

Constraints are the third part of your investment policy and are unfortunately the most binding in determining what investments are most appropriate for you. The questions of liquidity, your time horizon, tax considerations, legal constraints, and any other individual circumstances in your world that may affect your flexibility in investing all need to be addressed thoroughly. Once again, this need for caution underscores the importance and value of aligning yourself with a financial consultant who can outline the investing parameters specific to your circumstances.

The Importance of Investing

Stretching is important to a fitness routine because without it you are at risk of tearing muscles and limiting your physical performance during your workout. Why is it important to invest rather than to simply take your paycheque and deposit it into your bank account to earn 1% or 2% (or even less)? The obvious answer is that there is no reason to limit the performance of your money. In a workout, you don't want to limit your physical performance, so you take the time to stretch, warm up your muscles, and mentally prepare for the physical challenge. With your financial physique, the potential performance needs only to be recognized and outlined in order for you to initiate a financial plan. Perhaps right now you are convinced that you are unable to invest. Perhaps the thought of venturing into the market is too overwhelming for you. You may also believe that you do not have the purchasing power needed for successful investing. Take a look at the extremely inspirational chart on the next page.

Note that with an interest rate of 10% — a figure that a variety of investment instruments are capable of achieving — $48,000, invested in instalments of only $200 per month over 19 years, expanded to $148,566. The odds are pretty good

YEAR	ANNUAL CONTRIBUTION	REMAINING CAPITAL
1	$ 2,400	$ 2,640
2	2,400	5,544
3	2,400	8,738
4	2,400	12,252
5	2,400	16,117
6	2,400	20,369
7	2,400	25,046
8	2,400	30,191
9	2,400	35,850
10	2,400	42,075
11	2,400	48,922
12	2,400	56,455
13	2,400	64,740
14	2,400	73,854
15	2,400	83,879
16	2,400	94,907
17	2,400	107,038
18	2,400	120,382
19	2,400	135,060
20	2,400	148,566

that if you start this type of financial savings with $200 monthly, you will increase this amount. Therefore, your net amount will probably be over $200,000 if you add to your deposits "found" money such as tax returns, birthday money, job bonuses, and money that may be sitting in your bank account earning that 1% to 2%. The money is still liquid, meaning you can sell your holdings any time if you need access to these funds. However, as long as you do not need the money, you can increase its performance and ultimate value. Another point to remember is that this inspirational chart is based on a conservative estimate of a 10% return, so there is virtually no limit on the potential earnings as long as you choose the instruments wisely.

As we approach the millennium, it's becoming clear that the massive shift of equity from our parents to us is the greatest movement of wealth from one generation to the next in history. This unprecedented mass of money needs to be invested to maximize its value. Unlike in previous generations, there is no guarantee of government pensions to help subsidize our retirement. Currently, the federal government provides a pension to our senior citizens based on a percentage of their earnings generated during their employed years. However, that amount can be lessened depending on a retired individual's current income and amassed wealth. There are no guarantees even today that a retiring person will receive this pension, but the odds are considerably slimmer for the next generation. The money currently held in the Canada Pension Plan will be used up by the largest segment of our population, the boomers. When it is time for our generation to retire, we savvy investing Chicks will be the ones who are financially comfortable.

Also unlike preceding generations, the nuclear family with the male in the workforce as provider and the female at home as care giver is no longer the norm. Today there are many variations on family structure and gender roles, putting the financial responsibilities equally on both the male and the female. Women's social roles are continuously being redefined, whether as care givers to their children and parents *and* career professionals, or as members of either the baby boomer or Gen-X groups. The need for women to develop a healthy grasp of finance is absolute. Not only is the transfer of wealth of huge importance, but so is the fact that women are creating their own wealth in their careers. They need to ensure that the value of this money is maximized and outlasts them. It just does not make sense that we would work hard to graduate from school, develop a strong and fruitful career, and then lose direction and control of our wealth. By using Financial Fitness for Women, you can control the direction and performance of your hard-earned wealth.

LOOK TO THE FUTURE

When mentally stretching yourself to recognize your own strength, you should identify the various scenarios that could unfold in your future. As an independent career woman, your earning potential helps to define your future. Your financial fitness regime will help to structure your lifestyle. If you take the necessary steps to secure your financial fitness, you will have more opportunities available to you — you might want to invest in real estate, take special vacations, buy big ticket items such as a car or cottage, or just establish a sense of independence and security. By creating this source of power, you extend the boundaries of your world.

Once your financial fitness is established, you have empowered and improved yourself. Your sense of personal value will increase just as your investment portfolio has. This is not to say that your self-worth is measured by your financial status, but rather that your self-worth is measured by your independence and intelligence. Taking steps to ensure your own future and financial well-being enables you to reduce the stress in your daily existence.

Stretching ensures that your body is up to the task of exercise. Mental stretching ensures that you are up to the task of independence, financial freedom, and investment success. Until we acknowledge the power of female strength, we will be unsuccessful in our market participation. Once we accept our capabilities and unlimited potential, the financial fitness craze will take over the investment world in much the same way that women's enthusiasm has transformed the physical fitness industry.

At one time it was socially unacceptable for women to sweat. Our language reflected this taboo by referring to a women's sweat as "glowing." Now that the fitness industry is inundated with women who are bench-pressing, muscle-defined aerobics junkies setting physical goals that require sweat, mere glowing is no longer satisfactory. Likewise, women's infiltration of the investment world will be accompanied by changes in the way we use our language. Instead of the stereotype of women of the world talking about shopping and make-up over their lunch hour, the common Chick-speak will be about holdings and portfolio performance. Instead of sharing the name of a great nail technician, women will be passing on the name of a fantastic financial adviser to their friends so that they too can achieve financial fitness.

A stretch is the opening component of your workout because it is a cleansing process that opens your mind and body to new potentials. It also releases the negative toxins and doubts that can stifle your performance. Relaxation and regular breathing energize your body through oxidization, and the stress of the day is released. The muscles respond to this positive state, and you become more in tune with your body, and subsequently perform at a higher level. The same process can occur in your financial life, but you need to begin with a mental stretch in order to open your mind to new ideas. Female investment potential is huge — we make up more than half the population, and our numbers in the workforce are growing at a phenomenal rate. Women need only open themselves up to the investment world, and the barriers preventing financial independence will be broken down.

Women investors must acknowledge the importance of independence in financial fitness, and the value of keeping that independence. Should you meet a person with whom you choose to share yourself, fall in love, and create a partnership, congratulations! Falling in love and getting mushy and starry-eyed is a great part of being human. But you do not need to relinquish your financial fitness to someone else, no matter how mushy you get. Establishing your own investment identity is empowering. Relinquishing this power is not necessary in the equation of love. Financial details should not be a guarded secret in a relationship, but you do not need to hand over your financial plan to your partner. You might want to establish a joint account with your partner, but it is always a good idea to maintain your own financial plan and portfolio as well.

Perhaps your workouts have always been independent and you have created your own personal routine. But, after all, if you hire a personal trainer to rejuvenate your workout, or decide to participate in various aerobics classes, you do not need to throw away the old exercises that have served you well over the years. All that happens is that you incorporate some variety into your exercise regime. The same holds true to sharing your financial fitness routine. There is no need to release your independence and throw away your financial plan just because you have partnered up with the love of your life. Instead, perhaps a discussion with your financial adviser and your partner could result in a revised financial plan that would maintain your existing portfolio and also introduce a newer aspect of combined financial goals.

MATH = MONEY

The mental stretch is a tool used to increase women's financial confidence through an acceptance of our power and intelligence. To break down these barriers, we must become familiar with a very simple rule and follow it always: Math = Money. I don't mean to be insulting; rather, what I intend is to simplify and demystify. Had my teachers explained algebra and all those wonderful formulas and fractions in terms of dollars and cents, I guarantee that my attention level in math class would have been a lot higher. Think about how much more enjoyable math would have been if the message of financial independence had been delivered with it. Equations would have been easier to memorize if the end result of wealth were clearly understood.

In the past, female students were encouraged to excel in the arts and to leave the sciences to the boys in the class. That may have been less offensive in the days when our career choices were housewife or teacher. In today's world, math is a necessary subject for all students and if the message of Math = Money can be delivered more clearly, the likelihood of either gender developing poor financial habits will be lessened. As girls were predominantly steered away from mathematics, their passion for the financial markets has been understandably unexplored. With a mental stretch to accept that we do indeed possess the necessary mathematical skills to succeed in the investment world, that passion can be released.

A lot of men would participate in aerobics classes if they knew of the cardiovascular benefits. Initially, there is no problem attracting men to these classes (although I suspect that men show up at the classes simply because women are there!) but eventually their attendance wanes because they feel that aerobics classes are not a challenging enough workout and the choreography is complex. It's not that they don't work out or get cardio by other means, it's just that they completely miss out on the multiple benefits aerobics offers.

That is the message I am delivering on investing. It isn't that women are not capable of earning and saving, but they are limiting the performance of their funds by not participating in the markets and various investment instruments. You could run on the treadmill for hours, miles, and days without ever achieving your workout goals. It doesn't mean that you are not exercising; it just means that you are not maximizing your efforts to their absolute potential. In the same way, women are earning more, saving more, working incredibly hard to reach their career goals, and then losing control of their power by putting their money into bank accounts. The choice is made out of habit and a fear of the unknown.

Bolster Your Self-Confidence

There you are, lying on the mat in a corner of the gym yearning for your yin and yang to balance and for your breathing and pulse rate to settle down. The day has successfully beaten you up and your stress level has just reached a new high. In this frame of mind you arrive at the gym intent on increasing your flexibility level to that of an elastic as opposed to a tree. Now go ahead and put all those antagonistic thoughts of the day aside and just relax and stretch. Not going as well as imagined? Not surprising.

The same situation occurs in the mental stretch because of conflicting beliefs. It is not possible to automatically switch from one state to another without a pause for adjustment. Society has not had enough time for an adequate pause to accept women earning and handling money, or for women to accept and encourage each other's successes. Society has always accepted that men handle money matters, and women for the most part are the docile care givers who raise families but don't know anything about finance except how much grocery money has been provided. Now women are "bringing home the bacon, frying it up in the pan" and this needs to be acknowledged. Once women get comfortable with their own successes, they will not be so hesitant to develop market and investment savvy. Stop wrestling with the old social standards; it is time to stretch the definition of what women can do and increase the social acceptance of all that women accomplish.

Another important virtue of stretching before you work out is that you will avoid ripping, ruptures, and injuries. Investing without confidence can result in the most painful kind of injury — loss of capital. Investing without confidence means investing in ignorance. A proper workout stretch relaxes all the major muscle groups, so the mental stretch must deal with all the major success areas. Advancements in education, career, and family supports — and women's now proven ability to successfully balance all three areas — have placed women in a position to pursue equality and success. Once we've recognized these advances, we must review them frequently to continuously remind ourselves of our accomplishments. The more we can ease into a comfortable acceptance of our capabilities and strength, the more receptive we will be to a new concept.

The mental stretch will enhance the pride you take in your accomplishments and successes. Instead of limiting your investment potential with a mental crutch that debilitates you because of your gender, break down the limiting barriers with a mental stretch that allows you to develop pride in yourself and your gender. Armed with your self-confidence and pride, you will have a substantial impact on your own financial potential, and influence the other women in your life such as your daughters, sisters, mothers, friends, and co-workers. Thus you will have stretched your viewpoint to encompass the magnitude of all your present-day successes, opening your mind to new areas of challenge.

Perhaps you have recently taken time out of the working world to focus on family responsibilities. Not only have you interrupted your career path, earnings, and retirement plan contributions, but you are probably also going through a psychological adjustment. Your new lifestyle and daily schedule are completely different and although what you are doing now is no less valuable than what you were doing before, you are probably wrestling with a loss of professional responsibility and career duties.

The financial fitness workout can bring about a new source of empowerment and a new challenge to your daily routine. Although you may still crave adult interaction and the social interactions of the professional environment, through the mental stretch you will now be able to handle the family investment portfolio, look into various tax-efficient strategies for young families, learn about post-secondary education costs and how to save for them, maximize the family budget, analyze your cash-flow situation, and overall improve the financial performance of your family.

Once you see the many possibilities open to you in your present situation, you will begin to enjoy the way your daily routine has changed. You will realize that you have more time to focus on the financial aspects of your life, more time to consider the performance of your portfolio holdings. Ideally, you will recognize that you are now much more adept at handling financial details.

In physical terms, you can sit on the couch whining about your fitness level (or lack thereof) while stuffing potato chips into your mouth, or you can get up, stretch your body, and begin to achieve your fitness potential. Even if that potential represents a brief walk around the block today, at least it is a start.

SETTING GOALS FOR SUCCESS

To begin the mental stretch, you must identify your personal and financial goals, both short and long term. An example of a personal goal is the purchase of a real estate property; maybe you don't want to rent an apartment for the rest of your adult life or maybe you would like to ensure a future source of income from a rental property of your own. In order to achieve this goal, you meet with a financial adviser and devise an investment plan that will help you attain it.

Let's say you may have a set amount of money available for investments, and in the short term you need it to have grown to a specific amount (e.g., the down payment for a house).

Because you have made it clear you are not willing to lose more than 5% of your assets and since the time frame is short, the financial adviser recommends some rather aggressive equity investments that offer strong potential without a lot of risk. At the end of the time period, you withdraw the amount needed to purchase your property. Any leftover money can be used to maintain your investment account with your financial adviser — after all, your goal was achieved, so why not set a new one?

Another example of a financial goal is that of your registered retirement savings account. Perhaps you would like to be able to stop contributing to your RRSP at the age of 35, and from that point on let compound interest do its work, along with any corporate group RRSP contributions you make through work. At the age of 23, you have just started your first job since you earned your master's degree, so you set out to meet with a financial adviser. You recognize that time is precious, and the faster you get started on this registered savings plan, the sooner you will be able to let time handle the portfolio's growth. Your financial adviser instructs you to make the highest monthly contributions you can afford and make up the difference with an RRSP loan every year until you are 35. By following this plan, you will have reached your financial goal within your specified time.

Choosing a Financial Adviser

Once you have identified these goals, you may be unsure how to maximize the performance of your money in order to achieve your goals. You can begin the task of education through the services of a professional financial adviser, the

Internet, and books. How do you find the financial adviser best suited to you and your investment needs? The best advice I can offer is to shop around, armed with a list of questions that account for your specific investment needs. Have an idea of the types of answers you are looking for — avoid the slick and practised answers! Your adviser should be someone who listens to you, understands you, tells you the type of information you want to hear in answer to your questions, and teaches you more. Make sure that your personalities work well together, and that you are comfortable with the financial consultant you choose.

Keep in mind that you will be discussing very personal matters with this individual, such as your savings history, your salary, financial burdens, and future aspirations. If you do not feel comfortable with your financial consultant, your future financial fitness could be hindered. Also remember that you are the client, and that you should be treated well. All too often when women find themselves in situations in which they are not particularly well versed, they have a tendency to become intimidated and compliant. Your financial fitness relies on your being strong, confident, and aggressive in obtaining the ideal financial adviser.

If you were shopping around for a personal trainer and you acknowledged your need for authority to force you to exercise, you would not choose the friendly, bubbly fitness trainer who works at your gym. Rather, you would search out a drill sergeant type with previous training as a Navy Seal so as to ensure your dedication. Similarly, when you're looking for a financial consultant and, for example, you admit a weakness for withdrawing money, you need to align yourself with a professional who can point out the potential performance of funds and the problem of deducting from your present portfolio, and inspire you to leave the money in the portfolio. You need someone who is not afraid to communicate with you, someone who recognizes your character and tendencies.

A personal trainer is an individual you pay by the hour to help discipline you and create a time-efficient workout that deals with areas of concern you have about your workout. The trainer's knowledge of your lifestyle and goals combined with his or her kinesiology knowledge will deliver the results you crave from your workout. There is no mandatory rule stating that you must hire a personal trainer, but if you feel somewhat frustrated with your present workout or if you feel you could benefit from a professional's input, a personal trainer is the best bet to increase the productivity of your fitness regime.

A financial adviser can help you achieve your goals in a more efficient manner by introducing his or her professional knowledge and influencing your decisions. Perhaps you have been handling your investments on your own, or perhaps you are just starting out and professional guidance would help you to find the best financial plan and the best investment instruments available to you.

Paying for an investment adviser is not quite as simple as paying for your personal trainer. The investment community offers a variety of payment methods; as a Chick-A-Boom investor, it is imperative that you are familiar with all payment options before meeting with a financial adviser. Commission-based transactions are the main way financial advisers generate their salaries. Commissions are usually based on a percentage of the total transaction cost. Here's an example of how this works:

Janet wants to purchase 100 shares of Coca-Cola at $66 each. The total cost of this transaction is $6,732, because of a 2% commission charge.

100 shares at $66 =	$6,600
2% of $6,600 =	$ 132
Total Transaction Cost =	$6,732

One problem with being charged commission is that your average cost will be increased to absorb the commission charge. Another problem is that commission payments can be floating rates: the adviser has discretion when deciding what the client will be charged. An example of this is with mutual funds that have a commission or load (mutual fund industry jargon). These can range between 1% and 5%, and the adviser can decide how much within that range to charge the client.

The financial industry used to be covered in a blanket of opaqueness that concealed this type of discretionary control over a client's commission charges. The result was a monopoly on information. Through technological advancements, such as media and Internet accessibility, the concealing blanket has been replaced by transparency. Financial advisers should exercise a strict business philosophy based on the betterment of clients, as clients are now much better armed with knowledge of how commissions are generated and why. Should advisers not adhere to a philosophy of making the best decision for the client, the well-educated and well-informed client will fire the adviser faster than you can say "Chick-A-Boom!"

Financial advisers can also be paid through a fee-based operation. This is a great method for all parties concerned as it takes the commission conversations out of the relationship. The fee is an annual charge, the calculation of which is based on the total assets (amount of money) your investment account is worth. The industry norm is between 1% and 2%, and usually includes a base number of transactions for the year (for example, 20 trades in one year are included in the fee; the client has to pay an additional fee for more transactions). The best way to decide how to pay your financial adviser is to shop around and compare the numbers. If you feel you can competently handle your own investment portfolio, go ahead and do so. Just ensure that you have enough time to dedicate to your investment portfolio and know that your education level and familiarity level are appropriate. If you do not feel confident enough to do it on your own, the best route is to align yourself with a financial adviser, whether you have $100 or $1,000,000 to invest.

Ideally, your financial adviser will be in your life for a long time, and will influence all aspects of it. Never forget that just as you sought out and hired this individual, as the client you can also fire your financial adviser if you feel that he or she is not handling your portfolio in a manner that reflects your investment objectives. After all, you are the client.

WOMAN: THE GREAT INVESTOR

As your understanding develops, so too does your portfolio's substance and the complexity of investment choices that you make. And just like a fitness routine, the more you focus on your investing, the more addicted and dedicated to your goals will you become. You will be less inclined to throw your money away and more in tune with the goings on of the business world. The evening news will become multi-dimensional because you will see that some events have a bearing on the holdings of your portfolio, and your grasp of the world that surrounds you will be that much broader.

The catch-22 most women find themselves in is that they do not know much about the investment world and are too embarrassed to approach a professional with their questions, thereby limiting their ability to improve their financial situation. The financial fitness workout provides the basics you need to conquer your fears and succeed in building up your investments. As information gatherers, women tend to hold back until they have acquired and digested all the facts. Conversely, men tend to jump into the stock market, basing their decisions on sexy stock stories they hear by word of mouth.

Do you remember your first visit to the gym, when you walked around, taking inventory of all the machines and what they did? Next came a fitness appraisal in which an appropriate program was developed for you, based on your goals and physical condition. From that point on, your comfort level with your workout and your surroundings grew. That independence and self-reliance is a direct product of education and experience. As soon as we discover that initial confidence, our aggressive nature takes over and we want to increase the challenge and level of difficulty.

The reason for women's slow start in the investment world is a mystery. Granted, in the 1950s the lack of female participation in the market was not very puzzling. But today we should expect to see equal participation in the marketplace, considering there's nearly equal representation in most other social and economic areas. Women have fabulous investing advantages: we are information gatherers, more conservative than men, and goal oriented by nature. An application of these characteristics to investment strategies is both logical and advantageous. Yet instead of picking up the pace by initiating a successful investment process, most women are intimidated by the entire financial industry and, furthermore, are still averse to the perceived risk involved. Women need to establish self-confidence, which should be an obvious by-product of their education, professional careers, and personal accomplishments. Successful experience results in confidence and a more adventurous attitude towards former "unknowns." With this solid base, any number of goals can be set and met, whether you're concentrating on health or wealth.

KNOW THE DANGERS . . .

When risk is confronted and accepted a full mental stretch will occur. As information gatherers, women do not normally enter into a situation without acknowledging all possible outcomes. To recognize every possibility, all levels of risk must be addressed. You cannot blindly enter into the investment world as a new participant without first realizing your potential losses. If you avoid and deny the possibility of risk and loss, you are not adequately prepared to enter into the world of investing. When you consider the profit potential of becoming a shareholder in a publicly traded company, the upside looks great. But you don't truly appreciate the labours of your chosen company until you experience value loss. It isn't until the stock drops in price that you really understand the risk involved in your investment decision. When you lose money, your appreciation of risk escalates to the level of a seasoned investor, and you mentally exceed the barriers of a market novice. A clear example may help illustrate the value of acknowledging and understanding risk.

Cathy is a 30-year-old marketing manager who has an annual salary of $50,000. After budgeting for her rent, car expenses, food and entertainment, corporate RRSP contribution, and various monthly bills, she has $1,400 per month available for investing. She has decided to increase the potential performance of her money, and so has hired a financial consultant. Together they will work towards increasing her net worth. She opens an investment account at her financial institution and decides that in order to maximize her purchasing power and money performance, she should be aggressive in her speculation and risk-tolerance levels.

Her initial investment is in a start-up Internet company that is promising great things through its various press releases about upcoming deals and alliances. There is great risk associated with this company, but Cathy and her adviser decide that the potential gains far outweigh the possibility of loss. Cathy buys 14,000 shares of "internetinvestingcompany.com" at $0.40 per share. Including a commission of 2%, the trade total is $5,712; she has $4,600 in her account. She assures her financial consultant that the cheque with the $1,112 difference is in the mail, and the trade is executed. Much to her chagrin, the stock drops one day later to half its value when she bought it. Now instead of owing $1,112 on a market value of $5,712, she owes $1,112 on a market value of $2,800. Not only has she incurred a loss, she has also left herself in a very uncomfortable position of owing money on a money-losing investment.

This example illustrates the importance of allocating your assets and clearly outlining your loss potential and risk level. You must mentally prepare yourself (that is, stretch yourself mentally) so that you can account for all potential outcomes. Perhaps if Cathy had considered how quickly her money could evaporate from a portfolio that is invested in only one holding, she might have given more thought to diversification and not have put all her eggs into one basket.

Cathy's relationship with her financial consultant is obviously not well structured around her needs and goals. Her consultant failed to provide her with adequate guidance on her investment choice, and her commission charge did not decrease, even though Cathy herself had presented the idea to her adviser, and not the other way around. If you are going to develop a successful relationship with a financial consultant, you should ensure that honesty, clarity in communication, and trust are the bases of the relationship. Mental stretching is not about scare tactics, but rather about opening your eyes to all the potential outcomes, both good and bad.

. . . But Keep an Open Mind

Have you ever noticed that when you start to stretch, your level of flexibility is limited, or at least it appears to be? Stretching only really works to increase your flexibility once the mind relaxes and the body is free to increase its capabilities without the mental walls of negativity restricting performance levels. In this way, women can master the world of investing once they establish a positive, assertive confidence towards investments. All you need is an open mind about the brand new world of economics, investment, and money. The market is enticing and the energy of the investment world is undeniable. Yet women seem unable to shake the anxiety associated with investing. Fear of the unknown should not keep you away from your dreams, success, and independence.

When you stretch your body before a workout, your muscles get warmed up and subsequently become elongated, and you challenge and increase your flexibility level. The mental stretch serves a similar purpose: it elongates the potential of your money by encouraging the development of a positive female attitude towards investing. The mental stretch is a quick exercise in empowerment. Now that you are armed with a positive attitude towards financial success, your first step in the financial fitness workout is complete.

2

WARM · UP

Warming Up to the Idea
That a Woman's Place
Is in the Market

O kay, you pick up the morning paper from the front door, pour a coffee, and open your mind to a new day. You update yourself on both the local and international daily news. Deny it if you must, but there is usually a loyal glance at the horoscope section and then a brush through the sports. HELLO! What has been missed and, more importantly, why?

The business section is a fabulous read, but unfortunately the majority of chicks do not often appreciate it. Don't let that compressed bunch of numbers clumped together in hard-to-read print intimidate you. The market is a wild and wondrous place filled with terms and mannerisms not found anywhere else. Don't forget that math is all about money, and the investment world is merely the place where money is manufactured and moved about. The how and why of business, specifically what factors influence growth and what decisions lead to failure, are as fascinating as any soap opera ever was. Each company is made up of individuals who make decisions that can create a lot of growth or loss within your portfolio. As you delve into the world of finance, following the daily events of these businesses becomes highly addictive.

As I mentioned earlier, the participants in the investment world are predominantly male. The financial world is a male-dominated, technical arena that does not encourage inquiries, and therefore women rarely approach it. But that said, women *do* want to maximize their monetary power.

Financial marketers realize that although they know women's investment styles differ from those of the traditional male market, they don't know what the differences really are. Their approaches to women often don't translate into developing client relations despite women's burgeoning investment interest and power. Perhaps the mystery of connecting to female investors is solved simply by educating and introducing them to the concept of investing. Once an introduction is made and education is supplied, financial marketers will find that the female population will certainly make up for lost time as they explore their investment prowess.

As a new participant in the world of investing, you shouldn't worry about always being able to explain the economic cycles and monetary moves — not even the experts can do that. But when you have completed the financial fitness workout, following the business world will be an exercise in personal interest and focus. Once you understand a few absolutes of investing, you'll find that a woman's place is indeed in the market. You'll reach a comfortable level of understanding through this chapter, the Warm-Up section of the financial fitness workout.

Currently, the financial world markets its message predominantly to the male population, not because of intentional disregard for the female investor, but rather because of an old mindset that identifies financial purchasing power in the hands of males. Women need to be approached and encouraged to enter the investment world; financial institutions would be well advised to start producing advertising aimed at women.

The material that currently introduces an individual to financial markets is not geared towards women. We need to understand the investment arena in terms that make sense to us. The investment world uses sports metaphors and golf analogies to help introduce investment concepts to male investors, but comparisons that are easily understood by women also need to be provided. Different messages hit men and women differently. An example would be a bank commercial that presents a series of rapidly moving pictures showing the hustle and bustle of Bay Street and the competition encountered in the scramble for the top rung of the ladder. This type of advertising would directly appeal to a young urban male, whereas the same underlying message would be better delivered to a female audience through the use of smiles and images depicting strong customer service and proficient delivery. At the same time, the message must never lose the atmosphere of a safe and proven institution, as these are the archetypes that women will respond to.

Similarly, when an invitation of sorts is sent out to women investors, the message should be one of how investing can help you achieve goals and luxuries in areas such as family, travel, home, and entertainment. To the female mind, dollar signs do not represent success as much as a well-rounded lifestyle, although you can argue that they are basically the same means to an end.

Investing provides independence and security; it leads you to self-empowerment. Your confidence and dreams will grow at the same pace as your portfolio. I am not trying to send a message of materialism — no matter who you are and what your value system is, you can't deny that financial security is a comfort. This is especially true for women; they live longer and earn less money, two fabulously powerful incentives to increase their personal wealth. When you need no longer focus on how to meet your monthly bills, your career has advanced, and you are financially mature, your personal development is a lot easier to attain.

The Chick in Chick-A-Boom is a woman of substantial means and/or growing assets who does not need to worry about smaller concerns such as monthly payments, but rather focuses her concerns on the future (which, by the way, is a far more intimidating prospect than a mere phone bill). She can concentrate on her long-term goals because she has taken the necessary steps to organize her financial world; she has recognized that Math = Money, and with each paycheque she strengthens her position and potential. If you budget to create a financial plan that helps you arrive at even $100 a month after expenses, you have already taken the necessary steps to warm up and acknowledge that your place is in the market. You should be congratulated no matter what level you are at, as long as you have been responsible enough to initiate the creation of a financial plan.

GETTING FIT FOR THE MARKET

Financial fitness can be measured in exactly the same way as physical fitness. You don't need to worry about coughing up a lung or passing out during a marathon if you have been training and building up your strength and stamina. Once you have taken an introductory step class and built up the basic moves, you don't walk into the aerobics studio fretting over the potential of a broken ankle. Rather, you look forward to a cardiovascular workout with challenging choreography and great music, and to a fantastic mental and physical attitude at the end of the class, because you took the time to learn. You become more open-minded about risk taking and increasing personal challenge, and focus less on the negative potential outcomes.

Similarly, once you have learned the basics of investing and have seen your initial investments grow at a reasonably conservative pace, you are no longer concerned about losing all your money in a market you don't understand. You do not focus on minimal living expenses and meeting the monthly mortgage requests, rather you set your expectations on increasing the value of your portfolio and perhaps becoming more diversified. As you warm up to the fact that a woman's place is now in the market, your curiosity and investment expertise cannot help but grow.

A physical fitness workout begins with a stretch followed by a warm-up. A physical warm-up increases the blood flow and raises the heart rate slightly. You introduce some moves and practise them, but not at the same intensity as during your main cardiovascular workout.

The warm-up part of the financial fitness workout introduces and explains the basic terminology and activity of investing, but not at the same level as professional discussions and weathered traders' terminology.

WARM UP TO STOCKS

The best place for a basic introduction to investing is the newspaper. All the information you need is found in your local newspaper. Once you understand what stocks are, the newspaper will be a great resource for your investment decisions. Suppose you are interested in purchasing stock. The only thing holding you back from doing so is that you aren't altogether confident that you understand what stocks are or what they represent. No need to blush with embarrassment — keep in mind that there was a day when you didn't know what a grapevine was in an aerobics class, and that there was a time you didn't even know how to walk, let alone pace yourself properly for a 10-kilometre race! Just as with fitness, you need to understand the basics of finance before you can increase your performance.

Stocks — also referred to as shares — are individual pieces of a company that are sold to the public by the company as a means of raising money. You can buy common or preferred shares; depending on your investment objectives, you would choose either type. As a shareholder, you own a piece of the company; you have rights, such as voting at the annual shareholders' meeting and deciding on various matters that affect the profitable operation of the company. Obviously, a shareholder wants the profits to be maximized.

Now that you possess a working definition of shares and stocks, it's time to go back to the newspaper to follow your investment performance. The business section summarizes the market activities from yesterday's closing prices. Stocks are listed alphabetically and by the market they trade on. Although there are 27 exchanges in North America, it is usually just the major markets that are listed in the newspaper. The major markets include the NASDAQ Composite (NASDAQ), the Dow Jones Industrial Average (DJIA), the Toronto Stock Exchange (TSE), the Vancouver Stock Exchange (VSE), the Montreal Stock Exchange (MSE), and Standard and Poor's 500 (S&P 500). Each of the exchanges has its own symbol just as a company's stock does. Various investment instruments are traded on various exchanges, but for the purpose of this warm-up, the main focus will fall on equities (stocks and equity-based mutual funds) and bonds. When you turn to the stock listings in the business section, the companies will be arranged in a specific order that reflects particular statistics. The following headings are common in any newspaper available in North America:

52-Week									Vol		P/E
High	Low	Stock	Sym	Div	High	Low	Close	Chg	(100s)	Yield	Ratio

No need to panic — this is a dress rehearsal. By the end of this warm-up, you will be familiar with these abbreviations and the terms they stand for and will know how to read the stock pages like a seasoned ticker-tape professional. (Ticker tape was used to print out the market prices and trading floor activity but has since been replaced by computer screens.)

52-Week High and **52-Week Low** are self-explanatory: they represent the highest and the lowest values of the commodity over the last full year as of that date. These are the highest and lowest prices that the stock was bought at and sold for this past year. This is a very handy piece of information to refer to as it can provide you with a range to compare today's price with. It's important to know this information to ensure you are not paying too much for the stock.

Stock is the full company name.

The **Symbol**, or ticker, is an abbreviation assigned to the full company name by the market. For example, the full company name Coca-Cola is known to the New York Stock Exchange by the symbol KO.

Div is the dividend, an amount paid out of a company's profits to its shareholders. A simplified explanation of dividends is that they are a reward paid to preferred shareholders for investing in the company. You won't always find a value in this column as there is no legal obligation for a company to pay dividends.

High is the highest price the stock hit that day, and **Low** is the lowest price that day. These important figures will help you determine the volatility of the stock. If a stock has a low of $5 and a high that same day of $25, the odds are that something radical has occurred to that company today, and as a Chick-A-Boom investor you would perceive the volatility and look more closely for the reason behind the price fluctuation.

Close is the final trade and closing price of the stock.

Chg is the change in the value of the stock expressed in dollars, from the opening price to the closing price during the day's trading activity.

Vol is the volume of stock that was traded — how many shares were exchanged between buyers and sellers. The higher the volume, the more "liquid" your purchase is — that is, with a strong volume you can feel confident there are buyers out there should you want to sell your stock.

Yield is the return on the investment, expressed as a percentage, and is a great tool for every investor to use in order to understand portfolio changes and evaluate potential investment performance.

As an example of yield, let's look at real estate investment trusts (REITs). They are partly like a mutual fund, because the REIT is like a basket that holds various real estate properties, and partly like a stock, because it trades on the market. The yield on REITs is usually between 8% and 12%, which is considerably higher than the provincial savings bonds, which currently offer 4.5%. This product would be considered a decent alternative to fixed income products such as bonds because of its high yield.

The **P/E Ratio** (price earning ratio) is a means of comparing similar common stocks and is used by investors to test the quality and value of a company. The number value has been calculated by dividing the price of a stock by its earnings per share. This shows the value in the stock, and you can use this number to compare similar companies in similar industry sectors in order to find the company with the best stock price for you.

Taken together, these numbers represent the daily activity of any one company on the market. Now that you know how to interpret this information, you can base your investment decisions on knowledgeable answers. Let's read the stock performance of a hypothetical company, Company X. Once you're familiar with the format of the business pages, reading this information will be as natural as tying up your running shoes and filling up your water bottle!

52-Week									Vol		P/E
High	Low	Stock	Sym	Div	High	Low	Close	Chg	(100s)	Yield	Ratio
14.60	8.80	Company X	CX	0.12	10.00	9.85	9.95	−0.05	1587	1.2	8.5

Assume that this information on Company X is listed in the newspaper for September 16, based on the market activity for September 15. The high this year for the stock price was $14.60, and its lowest price was $8.80. The stock is the company's full name, in this case, Company X. The symbol assigned to Company X's stock is CX. The dividend offered on the preferred shares of CX is 0.12, meaning you will receive $0.12 on an annual basis on each share of CX that you own. The day's highest trade on CX was $10.00 per share, and the lowest trade was at a price of $9.85. The final price at the close of the market was $9.95. The change in the stock's price was -0.05. This means that the closing price on September 14 was $10.00, and as such there was a drop of $0.05. The volume, the total number of shares of Company X traded, was 1,587,000 shares. The yield offered by Company X is 1.2%, and the P/E ratio is 8.5.

As you can see, Company X did not finish off the day in a positive state, closing down $0.05 from the opening price. The value of the stock lost 5 cents in one day. This is not to say that Company X is a bad investment, because a buy or sell in the market should not be based on one day's performance. As the saying goes, it isn't timing the market, but time in the market that results in good performance. Females are recognized as being more apt to invest for the long term, so this mantra fits well with their investment philosophy. If the negative performance continued and the holding lost money more often than it made money, you would want to research any recent news on the stock that might be influencing its performance, and be prepared to sell off the holding if there seemed not to be much hope for a turnaround.

Building on the Basics

Now that you have read the flashing instructions on the screen of the StairMaster, you think to yourself, "What exactly does this mean and how is it going to affect my pursuit of physical fitness?" You see others' successful use of the treadmill yet feel sure you will end up flat on your face, getting tread marks on your nose. The same goes for this financial warm-up: it seems to make sense, and yet you wonder how exactly you are going to apply this to your life and financial goals. Quite simply put, it is all about personal philosophy and strategic planning. The StairMaster has programmed routines that you can initially follow until you have mastered those levels. At that point you can increase the challenge and redirect the workout to apply specifically to your goals. The treadmill starts off at a walking pace so that racing stripes on your face are not part of your ensemble, then increases in speed and incline.

With the investing information you are learning through the financial fitness workout, you can begin with the basics, such as stock-reading instruction, then build up to co-planning your initial investment strategy with your financial adviser. Strategic planning and personal philosophy tie closely together with financial planning and goals, and as you achieve each of the goals you have set, you recognize your achievements and set new levels to aim for.

You achieve your initial financial goal, such as starting an RRSP account. All of a sudden you have entered the financial world. You are one of the players, and surprisingly it is not as frightening as you thought it would be. So you advance to a new financial plan — maybe you want to aim to open a cash account so you can also invest *outside* of your registered account. After diligently contributing a few hundred dollars to your RRSP on a monthly basis, you realize that you have some excess cash available at the end of every month. Now you decide to open a cash account, fulfilling your financial goal. Through the successful completion of each goal, you provide yourself with increased self-confidence and empowerment, and you develop a hunger for investing and expanding your financial goals, both long and short term.

CHANGING ROUTINES FOR CHANGING GOALS

As I said earlier, the best warm-up is merely a light preview of the actual cardiovascular workout coming up. Your investment strategy is similar in that it is a sample of your investment philosophy. Part of your strategy is to determine your asset allocation — that is, how you divide the assets in your portfolio into three different categories: cash, fixed income, and equity. Cash refers to completely liquid assets (i.e., savings in a bank account). Fixed income instruments are promises made to investors to receive money at specific times (i.e., bonds and

Guaranteed Investment Certificates (GICs)). Equity is defined as stocks and equity-based mutual funds.

Asset allocation reflects your investment strategy based on risk and reward. It involves various factors such as age, monetary wealth, debt, family status, and goals. You are developing a plan to reach your goals, so you need to look at every aspect of your financial life.

Debra provides our first example of how to develop asset allocation. As a 25-year-old who was establishing herself in the advertising industry, her annual salary was $32,000 and her expenses left her with $200 per month to put towards an investment account outside of her registered retirement plan at work. She contacted a financial adviser whom she had met with once when she was initially shopping around and interviewing different brokers, and arranged a meeting. At the meeting, the financial adviser worked with Debra and established an asset allocation appropriate for someone her age.

The adviser suggested a heavier weighting of Debra's portfolio in equity, because the younger the investor, the greater the risk tolerance. (The rule of the industry is to subtract your age from 100 to obtain the percentage of your portfolio that should be in equities. This rule of thumb is only a starting point. Through discussions with your financial adviser you will discover any specific considerations that may alter that rule of thumb, such as zero tolerance for loss — or perhaps at the other end of the spectrum, you might want to increase your exposure to equities and risk.) Debra decided on 75% equity exposure and 25% in fixed income. There was no reason for cash because she was contributing $200 every month, so there was always a guaranteed cash flow.

Your asset allocation is not written in stone. When Debra,

at 36 years old, met with the same financial adviser (no need to change if the individual is doing a good job, and the portfolio is growing at an acceptable rate according to your financial plan), she decided it was time to alter the asset allocation. Her risk tolerance had changed lately because she had started a family. She realized that her asset allocation needed to represent growth potential, but with an emphasis on safe instruments that could guarantee a particular return. Her money was now expected to cover her child's post-secondary education, not to mention any short-term expenses that might arise. Gone were the carefree days when Debra threw her portfolio into the volatility of the market and was comfortable with that risk level. Her asset allocation was altered to reflect her current lifestyle, and there was now more emphasis placed on fixed income. She felt that emphasizing conservatism would ensure the safety of her assets, but continuing to participate predominantly in equities would maximize the potential growth. So she decided to alter the asset allocation to a mix of 60% equities and 40% fixed income, with the equities weighted in preferred shares so as to ensure the dividend income, and the fixed income predominantly in corporate bonds to ensure a higher yield.

Continuing the observation of Debra's life, at 57 years of age, with her child in university and her mortgage fully paid, she began to weigh retirement options, and her investment objectives once again shifted. She is now focused on security rather than on increasing the size of her assets. Her RRSP and investment account need once again to be reviewed so that her risk tolerance adequately reflects her position in life. She needs to know that there is limited risk involved in the holdings of her portfolio. Planning for her retirement is now key and there is no room for error. She doesn't want her retirement years to be spent working part-time at McDonald's. Rather, she dreams of a schedule of travel, relaxation, perhaps half a year in the sun polishing up her golf and tennis games.

Therefore, when she reviews her portfolio's asset mix, she decides on a change from equities to fixed income. Debra is comfortable with a 5% to 10% return based on high-grade bonds; her assets will be safe and her growth will continue. Her equity weighting will shift to a more appropriate 35% level and her fixed income level will be increased to 55%. She decides that there is no need for a cash position as her savings account will provide her with the limited liquidity needed for her daily living expenses. She leaves the office of her financial adviser satisfied that not only are her assets going to continue to grow, but that she will be able to sleep at night knowing that there is limited risk associated with the money that will provide her with comfort during retirement.

No matter what your age, you should always be comfortable with the asset allocation set up in your portfolio. Make sure you can sleep at night, secure in the investment decisions you have made. Risk tolerance is not set in stone. Look at your exercise routine — what is comfortable for you and your level of fitness may not necessarily gibe with others in your age group. There are a lot of 20-somethings who are not adequately co-ordinated for — or simply do not enjoy — aerobics classes, just as there are 50-somethings who are more than happy to endure a high-impact hour-long class. It just depends on the individual and his or her comfort level.

Flexibility is needed to reassess both your needs and the current economic conditions in order to maximize the performance of your money. Asset allocation determines 92% of long-term results, and during periods of market volatility it can be a source of great comfort. The flexibility of your asset allocation is not only called upon during life-changing occasions, you can also rely on that flexibility in making short-term investment decisions.

For example: you have invested heavily in the stock market and your asset mix is 70% equity, 20% bond, 10% cash. During the past six months, the market has been hitting record highs, and you have been seeing fabulous returns on your investments. Seemingly out of the blue, your financial adviser calls you and suggests a rearrangement of your asset allocation. You question the radical move and ask for validation, especially with the capital gains you are seeing. Luckily, your financial consultant is dedicated to the industry fundamentals — keeping up to date on current events, research, yields, price, and value of a company. After listening to the argument that the market is about to spiral downwards, you decide to trust your consultant and rearrange your asset allocation to be slightly underweight in equities, with more emphasis on bonds and cash. The following week there is a tumultuous jolt on the Asian market and stocks across the board start heading down. Kudos to your financial adviser, and equal accolades to you for your flexibility in rearranging your assets.

This example of asset allocation is similar to readjusting your warm-up to accommodate a changing focus in the gym. Perhaps your workout is going to be geared to preparing for running a race. Your warm-up will no longer need to incorporate limbering up for weights, as the emphasis will be on cardiovascular training. However, once the race is done, you may want the option of returning to weights and improving your toning. The flexibility to change your emphasis is the key to success, both in health and wealth.

Gearing up to Warm Up

You find yourself tired of the paint-dry rate at which your money is increasing in your savings account, and you know of quite a few individuals who have earned a lot more through participating in the stock market. The only question is, how do you make the change, choose the companies, and start maximizing your money? There are four suggested sectors to divide your investment dollars into when dealing with securities: industrials, consumers, commodities, and interest-rate sensitive. The percentage allocation for each sector varies to reflect the current political, economic, and social situations that are influencing the market.

The **industrials** are a medium-risk sector; examples include high technology, transportation, and chemical companies.

The **consumer** sector is closely allied to the domestic economy, exposed to medium risk and is made up of retail, communication, healthcare, and biotechnology services.

Commodities — minerals and metals such as gold and silver — are a high-risk sector that moves with the world economy and is highly cyclical. The stock prices of the resource companies are very temperamental and susceptible to drastic movements, both up and down.

The **interest-rate-sensitive** sector usually has less price volatility and deals with companies such as real estate, financial services, pipelines, and utilities.

Warming up to the market also includes familiarizing yourself with a company's annual report. This report explains all relevant numbers, ratios and financial statements, corporate moves, and decisions that have occurred over the past fiscal year of operation. It's beneficial to be able to recognize strong performance numbers and growth opportunities within a company. While understanding an annual report will not lead you to expert predictions on the market, the skill will enhance your ability to make educated decisions about which companies to focus your attention on, and why. The annual report provides you with a corporate profile, financial highlights, future objectives, the financial statement, and a message from the president. These pieces of information, along with relevant news items, research reports, and your own interest in a company, can be combined to influence which companies you and your adviser choose for your portfolio.

You can request annual reports directly at the corporate head office of any publicly traded company. Usually the investor relations or public relations area of the company will put together an investors' package that also includes recent press releases and information on the company. Don't be afraid to request this kind of information, and remember that it is in the company's best interest to supply this information to interested members of the public, as that is where the investors are.

PICK UP THE PACE

It is imperative for women to warm up to the market, for only then can we hope to increase our own independence and financial power. Look for opportunities to increase your health and wealth in many different places. Perhaps your employer has an employer contribution plan, and you are not taking advantage of the opportunity to make your money work with theirs, maximizing your contribution power. An optional shareholder plan may exist but if you are not participating, you are missing out on dollar-cost-average investing and compounding interest opportunities galore.

Missing out on these opportunities is like working out for two hours, then noshing down a dozen doughnuts and some fries. You are dedicated to your exercise program, but fail to follow through to make the most of the performance outcome. Investing is exactly the same: you do not want to limit your potential performance by making short-term negative moves that could affect your long-term financial situation. An example is found in the workforce and the layoffs that affect so many of us nowadays. Downsizing can carry with it large chunks of cash that should be invested so as to maximize their value. But most people focus on the negative aspect of the situation — that they have lost their job and need to use the severance money to survive — therefore failing to meet the investment opportunity. The money in the severance package can be transferred into your RRSP as tax-free money that can be put to use immediately in your portfolio. Proper financial planning includes saving approximately three months' worth of wages as an emergency fund. Had you been caught in a corporate downsizing, you could have lived off your emergency fund and placed the severance package directly into your RRSP.

Tax credits that the government sends out are another ideal investment opportunity that most people simply overlook. Even the last time you withdrew money from your savings account and your budget was blown for seemingly no reason, you missed an investment opportunity.

Warming up to the idea of investing includes recognizing all opportunities to invest, as well as putting an end to both excuses and procrastinating. As a woman's place is now in the market, she had better get in there and prove it. There is neither a perfect time nor absolute amount needed to begin your career as an investor. There is no time like the present, though, and as long as you can spare a minimum of $100 a month, you can participate now. Do not hesitate any longer. Start with a minimum, then when your earnings accommodate greater participation, increase your investments. The longer you stay out of the financial world, the higher the risk that you will not have enough money to cover your retirement, let alone enough to provide you with the ability to achieve short-term goals.

3

CARDIO

Chick Picks, Cardio Blips,
and Market Activity

That heart-stomping, beat-thumping, adrenaline-rushing, endorphin-screaming high — how can you say no to such an energized state? Cardiovascular activity is the main component of your workout. You are maximizing your activity to challenge your heart rate and increase your oxygen exchange, with the end result of burning fat. Choosing a company in which to invest your hard-earned money, and then watching as the market moulds and manipulates the value of that stock is a true comparison.

When you purchase a stock, you become a part owner in the company, which leads to a more emotional response to the market's activity. All of a sudden, the ups and downs of the Dow and what value the dollar closed at are not just annoying interruptions babbled by the newscaster between the world news and sports. Now the financial activities in any given business week will interest you at a level of real comprehension — your money. And trust me on this, your resting heart rate will definitely be challenged occasionally during a prolonged time in the market.

The cardio portion of your workout is what all the other components build up towards. It is the meat of the workout and, if done properly, can make a fantastic difference in your physical condition. The stretch, warm-up, weights, and abdominals are all integral parts of the workout, but the cardio is the sexiest. Once again citing the similarities between health and wealth, it is hardly a surprise that hot stock stories are referred to as sexy.

CHICK PICKS

Chick Picks represent an innovative way of thinking about the stock market that is exclusively intended for women. Warren Buffett has a philosophy that the only companies worth investing in are those that you understand. He has built his company, Berkshire Hathaway, into a multi-billion-dollar enterprise with strict adherence to this investment philosophy.

Who better to design a portfolio of stocks that are easily identifiable and understood by women than women? With that premise in mind, Chick Picks can be best described as a portfolio of stocks representing companies that influence all aspects of the day-to-day lives of multi-dimensional modern women. This portfolio can be chosen by each individual female investor (with the professional guidance of her adviser), to reflect her social, economic, and political lifestyle. Once again there are four suggested sectors to divide your investment dollars into: industrials, consumers, commodities, and the interest sensitive.

INDUSTRIALS	**CONSUMERS**
High-Tech	Communication
Transportation	Healthcare
Chemical	Biotech
Environmental	Retail

COMMODITIES	**INTEREST SENSITIVE**
Metals	Real Estate
Mining	Pipelines
Oil and Gas	Utilities
Paper and Forest	Financial

Using the above chart for reference, it becomes quite easy to recognize the components in your life that represent companies worth investing in, and that you would therefore understand. For increased variety, think about the basic, luxury, and fantasy items and brands in your everyday routine. Look at the economic, political, and social patterns of today's headlines, and pay attention to matters that interest you and affect your life, either present or future.

The most obvious example of a sector that is headline-worthy is medical care as it affects both your present and future lifestyles. Changes in the understanding of health affect most generations; in particular, the elderly members of our society are better educated about proper diet and exercise than any other preceding generation, which in turn results in people living longer. The stock of pharmaceutical companies will continue to develop in step with the development of products that cater to the elderly. But to further the importance and value of this sector, pharmaceutical companies are also working on products that will affect several age groups. Examples of these include drugs to treat breast, colon, and other varieties of cancer; arthritis; AIDS; depression; osteoporosis; impotence; and heart conditions.

The more you can prepare, research, and offer up for discussion to your financial adviser, the more you will be able to participate in decisions about the make-up of your portfolio. Every economist and analyst out there has a different formula representing an ideal diversification of the four sectors. Every economist and analyst also has a benchmark asset allocation in regards to equities, bonds, and cash. The soundest advice that I can suggest is that you discuss with your financial adviser the best strategy for your investments.

Example 1 "A Day in the Life Of"
You may be looking for some domestic investment ideas and your day-to-day existence offers unlimited ideas:

Waking up in your new home just purchased from A.E. LePage (real estate = Interest Sensitive), you have a morning shower (hydro company = Interest Sensitive) and wash your hair with your Aveda shampoo (hair products = Consumers), dig through your medicine cabinet for a Tylenol (chemical = Industrials), then put on your favourite Revlon make-up products (retail = Consumers). You turn on the Sony stereo for the news (communication = Consumers), log onto your Dell computer to check your e-mail and do some personal banking (communication = Consumers, Internet = Industrials, banks = Interest Sensitive). You get dressed in your new Ralph Lauren suit (clothing = Consumers), read the paper (forest and paper = Commodities), take out the garbage (environmental = Industrials), and set the house alarm (high tech = Industrials).

You hop into your Ford car (transportation = Industrials), stop at the Petro Canada gas station (oil and gas = Commodities), then drive off to your shift at the hospital (healthcare = Consumers) where you have worked for the past two years as a nurse.

Example 2 "Exotic Flair"

If you were looking to introduce some foreign content into your holdings (your RRSP can have a maximum 20% foreign content; outside your RRSP there is no limitation), you could add some exotic elements to the exercise:

Rushing through the airport's new terminal to make your Air Canada flight (transportation = Industrials) to "foreign place," you stop to pick up a few incidentals at the magazine shop (retail = Consumers), check your flight information on the computer (high tech = Industrials), and board the plane (transportation = Industrials). You arrive in "foreign place" and check into the Four Seasons Hotel (tourism = Consumers). Taking a tour of the capital city, you notice a few of the major industrial players and their locations near the harbour, highways, and airport (transportation = Industrials).

The oil drills littered throughout the landscape (oil and gas = Commodities) offer an interesting backdrop to the ocean and the palm trees, and you notice that most of the citizens seem to be enjoying a healthy lifestyle, measured by the real estate boom (real estate = Interest Sensitive) and the abundance of new cars (retail = Consumers) on the road (transportation = Industrials). But as you sit on the tour bus assessing all of these economic factors, you smile and remind yourself that you are on vacation and the only thing you should be wondering is what level of SPF your Coppertone lotion (retail = Consumers) should have, and where you can buy a Coke (retail = Consumers) as this heat is a killer!

Example 3 "Kid's Play"

If you were interested in starting a college fund (in trust account) for a child in your life, you could spin a youthful twist on the exercise.

On a family trip to Walt Disney's theme park (communication = Consumers), driving down the highway and desperately searching for a gas station (oil and gas = Commodities), you question the sanity involved in your decision not to fly (transportation = Industrials). To keep Junior happy and quiet, you pass him his favourite Fisher Price toy, bought at Wal-Mart (retail = Consumers) the day before you left on this trip. You take a moment to dig through your Louis Vuitton purse (retail = Consumers) to look for your bankbook (financial = Interest Sensitive), and dial into the telephone banking service on your Nokia cell phone (high tech = Industrials). Junior starts wailing and feels a bit feverish, so you quickly reach for a thermometer to take his temperature (healthcare = Consumers). Thankfully he is not ill, just thirsty, so you reach for a Del Monte juice box (grocery = Consumers) and lean back in your seat, eagerly awaiting the welcoming sight of the park's entrance gate.

Example 4 "Guy Stuff"

Perhaps you want to develop a portfolio for that special man in your life (because you know that he will have kittens if your portfolio continues to outperform his!), so you focus in on male-dominated subjects and lifestyle matter.

Sunday afternoon, the Sony Trinitron television (electronics = Industrials) is blaring the NFL pre-game show (communication = Consumers), the Labatt beer (retail = Consumers) is cooling in the fridge (chemical = Industrials), and the telephone (communication = Consumers) is ringing off the hook with all the confirmations for this afternoon's get-together. The sports section of the newspaper (paper and forest = Commodities) is littered all over the carpet (chemical = Industrials) and you secretly hope that the resale value in the neighbourhood (real estate = Interest Sensitive) is not affected by all the hooting and hollering that is about to plague the area!

Example 5 "My Home = My Holdings"
Have you ever taken a really good look at what is in your home and how it is reflective of social patterns? Have you ever even considered that what society likes and dislikes influences the strength of the stock market? Nike is a perfect example. The kids love it, the athletes love it, the majority of aerobics and health club members sport the "swoosh" insignia on a daily basis. Even couch potatoes probably own a sweatshirt or two, as they are the most comfortable for lounging! The stock's value is a direct correlation of the popularity and market support that Nike receives from us. As an exercise, compare the stock price of Nike to Reebok, Adidas, or any other competitor within the sector.

Exxon is another example. Right after the oil spill in Alaska and the environmental disaster that ensued, the company's stock price plummeted. This behavioural pattern sends a strong message to the corporate world: In order to enjoy the successes of being a well-supported stock, you must operate in a manner that is responsible to your investing public.

The term "value stock" usually refers to the price of a stock compared to its potential price. Investors are able to buy at a discount in comparison to the stock's potential value. But perhaps the definition should be expanded to say that a value stock is equally defined by its ethical value and not just its monetary value.

Here is a sample of the types of items and services that can be found in your house, as you walk from room to room:

LAUNDRY ROOM

Laundry Products (detergent, softeners) INDUSTRIALS

Soap INDUSTRIALS

Electricity INTEREST SENSITIVE

BATHROOM

Appliances (washer, dryer) CONSUMERS

Towels CONSUMERS

Appliances (tub, sink, toilet) CONSUMERS

Pharmaceuticals CONSUMERS

Make-Up CONSUMERS

Vitamins CONSUMERS

Electricity INTEREST SENSITIVE

Cleaning Products INDUSTRIALS

KITCHEN

Groceries CONSUMERS

Appliances (fridge, microwave) CONSUMERS

Oil and Gas INTEREST SENSITIVE

Hydro INTEREST SENSITIVE

Furniture CONSUMERS

LIVING ROOM

Television CONSUMERS

VCR CONSUMERS

Stereo System CONSUMERS

Furniture CONSUMERS

The direct brand or company names mentioned in these examples are just that — examples. You're likely to choose different brand names to investigate for inclusion in your investment portfolio. I've used the ones I did just to provide general ideas or motivation for you, but only a financial adviser who knows the client and her objectives is able to give specific investment advice, and from there the individual investor needs to also contribute his/her opinion and choices. What this exercise can provide you with is an increased understanding of the investment world as it is incorporated into your world on a daily basis. Recognizing the investing opportunities that exist within your world and learning that the intricacies of the business environment coexist with your own life is key to becoming a successful investing Chick.

CARDIO BLIPS

Pushing yourself harder than ever before, you complete the session on the rowing machine, move onto the stationary bike, then go straight into the swimming pool to finish off your cardio with some laps. Welcome to your own personal triathlon, where motivation, health, goals, and success are all being measured internally through your heart rate or "cardio blips." Heart rate changes in the gym as a result of physical exercise are a good thing. Heart rate changes as a result of stock market movement are not always so positive. The best way to maintain a constant heart rate in association with your investing is through diversification and asset allocation. In plain speak, don't put all your eggs in one basket. If the market tanks and all your money is invested in stocks, a lack of diversification would be a recipe for poverty. But if the interest rates soar to new highs and the bond prices sink below ground level, you don't want to have all your money in fixed income.

Cardio blips occur when investors do not play by these rules. If a couch potato decides to run a 10-kilometre race because he sees a marathon race on television, the odds are pretty good that the potato's heart rate will be racing to dangerous new levels. But if that same person trained and prepared appropriately for the race, the heart rate would be a more controlled tool that could be used to measure the athlete's overall performance.

In the same way, market participation can be a training tool to help you attain your short- and long-term financial goals. If the proper asset mix is not in place, your portfolio's performance will not maximize your money's potential value. If you do not have the right asset allocation in the stock portion of your portfolio, you run the risk of "blowing yourself up." This is an industry term, and it is one of the most appropriately descriptive. Should you put all your eggs in one basket (by investing in one sector or stock), you are in a susceptible position, completely defenceless, and 100% dependent on the performance of that sector.

In 1997 a gold company named Bre-X caused a large number of investors to lose a lot of their money, portfolio earnings, real estate, and life savings. There was also a downward spiral in the mining sector as a result of this company's reporting procedures and misleading operations. The gold reported to have been found in the site was believed to be such a sure thing that some investors decided to decrease the range of their asset allocation, not only to increase their weighting in equities, but more specifically to increase their holdings of that one particular stock. Greed and excitement over-ruled the asset allocation, diversification, and quality investing that would reflect the investors' objectives and investment philosophies.

The downward shift in the resource sector is still being felt in our economy today. You need only look to natural resource sector mutual funds and their recent performance to see the truth of this observation. Gold used to be the common denominator in value, more so than any currency. This is no longer the case, and some of the cause for this switch away from gold can be traced back to the gold company scandal of 1997. It proved once again that proper asset allocation is the only successful way to invest.

The asset mix should be a flexible equation that can be restructured at any given time, to properly reflect the political and economic temperament existing both in the outside world and, more importantly, within your own. Look, for example, at a "dead cat bounce" (no offence to all you cat lovers out there — once again this is an industry term). A dead cat bounce occurs when the market drops, picks up a little, and then drops again, faking out investors and luring them into a false sense of security. A well-educated investor should be able to recognize this movement pattern, which is key to avoiding unnecessary losses.

Knowing what a company should be valued at is not difficult as long as the company is operating in a profitable and honest manner. You should not be lulled into a false sense of security on a particular holding if you have chosen quality stocks. The market value should reflect the operations, development, and earnings of the company. There should be proof in the annual report that validates the price of the stock. If you have invested in a company because of rumours you heard at the gym, or because the newspaper reported a record-breaking volume of trades on a company the day before, you are risking too much.

Value as a Vital Sign

Choosing companies to invest in is not an easy exercise. Your choices should reflect quality in the names of the companies that you want to own. Investing in quality will help you avoid dead cat bounces and other unnecessary risks.

Other than stating the obvious — long-term investing is the only answer to successful investing — the only other defensive move you can use to increase the protection of your investments is to diversify. Diversify your money into well-performing, strong brand-recognition, and strong value companies. As previously mentioned, value stocks are a combination of monetary and ethical value; socially conscientious corporate behaviour is definitely included in the monetary returns on a stock.

Suppose you are thinking about investing in Nike, but then learn about rumours that suggest Nike is responsible for child labour in a third world country. This bothers you so much that you refuse to invest a single cent into this company until you can be provided with concrete proof showing Nike does not participate in such poor corporate behaviour. (This accusation was actually made against Nike, but was subsequently proved false.) Alternatively, you find out that Nike has fitness facilities on all of their corporate sites and that there is a policy encouraging employees to make the most of their use of the facilities. This policy exists because Nike believes that the employees' productivity will be increased because of the positive effects of exercise. As you are a dedicated fitness enthusiast who also knows the positive effects of exercise, you decide to invest in this company, which reflects your own philosophy on fitness. These are clear examples of how your portfolio's asset mix can be influenced by the political, economic, and social world in which we live. It also demonstrates the power each individual investor possesses over the corporate world.

MONITOR YOUR HEART RATE

Equities are a sub-group of your portfolio that also requires diversification. Granted, stocks are quite exciting in comparison to watching your bonds come due. That is certainly not to say that fixed income is any less an important part of your portfolio, but for this part of the book the focus is on equity.

Have you ever been in the middle of an aerobics class? The music is loud and cranked up to about 140 b.p.m., your heart is pounding, your bright red face is offering a testimony to everyone as to how hard you are working, you can't decide if this a love or hate thing, but the one thing you know for sure is that you will absolutely not walk out!

The same is true for participation within the stock market. The market rises and falls to a power that's seemingly unknown and unexplainable. You wonder why you have put your hard-earned money into this crazy ride, yet at the same time you find the adrenaline and mental rush highly addictive. The potential upside is undeniably attractive, and if you have a professional adviser working with you, the risk tolerance and asset allocation that you have developed should offset the rocky times of volatility. Diversification reduces the overall risk of your portfolio and also increases your portfolio returns. Without this key element in times of volatility, your portfolio will take a mean beating. Think of investing in the stock market without diversification as the same as lifting weights and only working your left tricep and left trapezius muscles. Eventually you are going to walk crooked, look completely ridiculous, and risk injury as a result of being underdeveloped.

Heart rate monitors are used in health clubs and by athletes alike as a new training tool. The heart rate monitor is used to read and target your heart rate. The ideal target zone is identified and utilized as a tool to help you measure whether you are working too hard or too lightly, based on your age and current physical condition. The monitor also helps to ensure that you are effectively burning fat and working within your targeted heart rate zone. Asset allocation and proper diversification of the equity portion of your portfolio are analogous to a heart rate monitor. Ignoring the importance of research into your portfolio's holdings and failing to respect the risk associated with investing in the stock market is tantamount to giving yourself a financial heart attack!

Accounting for various market activities can be compared to using a heart monitor. As an example, let's say that gold prices drop. If you were weighted heavily in gold and mining, the heart rate monitor would blip and bleep like crazy as your net worth dropped. With proper diversification in all appropriate sectors, the monitor would simply recognize the minor blips in the market and coast through at a conservative, long-term investor's rate.

Increased diversification of your investments can also be achieved by investing in foreign markets. If the North American market entered into a serious bear market period, the investments you made in the European and Asian markets might help you during this negative performance period. If you don't feel very familiar with the foreign markets, speak with your financial adviser to learn about the various investment opportunities available. Some mutual funds are strictly composed of foreign holdings. You could also develop a strategy that reflects internationally sound business performers in such sectors as telecommunications, pharmaceuticals, or other consumer goods.

The more strategies you can familiarize yourself with, the more diverse your portfolio's holdings can be and thus the more secure your assets will be. In a similar way, the more variables you have available to your fitness routine, the better you will feel about dedicating yourself to achieving your fitness goals. If all you do is run, and then unfortunately you develop an ankle injury that keeps you from exercising, you will no doubt become frustrated because you can't exercise while you're healing. However, if you have a weight routine or a swimming program in your repertoire of physical activities, the inability to run for the next few weeks will not destroy your workout nor your drive.

Market activity that would encourage a steady heart rate pattern includes investing in health, because of the mass of ageing baby boomers and changing social attitudes in general. I can guarantee that I am not the only crazy one out there who wakes up before sunrise, grabs a suit bag, and cruises off to the gym to crank it out before a full day at the office. The reason for this is simple: not mental instability, but a desire for health and wealth. Increasing both your productivity and life span acts as an early riser incentive. Better health and an increased physical fitness level have become goals shared by people of all age groups, social standing, and gender. As a Chick-A-Boom savvy investor, you are able to recognize this important social trend as a promising, understandable investment opportunity.

The prescription drug industry is one area in particular that will definitely grow and develop in the next few years. The drug company Pfizer has helped to prove this. In 1998 it launched a product that revolutionized the boomer impact on pharmaceuticals and foreshadowed what the economy could expect because of the purchasing power of this social demographic group. The company's drug Viagra proved that boomers are willing to pay any amount of money to increase the quality of their lives. This product is not nearly as valuable to society as pharmaceuticals that will cure disease, reduce the incidence of cancer, and increase the quality of life for terminally ill patients, but look at the staggering sales Viagra has produced.

Breast cancer, osteoporosis, AIDS, various forms of cancer, and heart disease all seem to be claiming more victims as the fight goes on to develop cures. The companies that find the successful drugs will make a lot of money; as an investor in these companies, money would trickle down into your portfolio too. Healthcare will also be directing a lot of resources to senior housing, nursing, medical care, and the funeral industry as the majority of the population reaches retirement age. Once again, as a clever investing Chick, you would find this predictable social movement not only interesting but also a fantastic area of investment opportunity.

Chick Picks, as was earlier mentioned, is a continuously developing portfolio strategy that you can alter at any time. It's necessary to review and alter your strategy now and then as there are never any guarantees as to which company will be the market leader from one day to the next. Today it may be a safe bet that Bell is the telephone giant in Canada, so BCE is a fantastic stock to hold in your portfolio. But who is to say that land lines are not soon to become dinosaurs and that cellular phones and the companies that own them aren't tomorrow's fabulous stock? The science of choosing a strongly performing stock is based on research, market performance, strong company earnings, and development of innovative products that will keep that company a leader. The market activity that accompanies your choices will show you the importance of regulating the sector weightings and how sensitive the market is to various influential factors.

Just as aiming for a training zone on a heart rate monitor can aid in strengthening your athletic condition on a long-term basis, in a portfolio, proper diversification can aid in the development of long-term gains and wealth.

4

STRENGTHENING

Cross-Training Investment Products — Time Is Muscle

Cross-training as an additional component of your workout? Isn't it enough that you drag your sorry bag of bones to the gym as often as you do? Isn't it enough that you participate in an aerobics class and occasionally attempt weights in those pump classes? How much time do you really have to spare to increase the overall structure of your workout? Cross-training . . . How the heck are you supposed to successfully achieve that?

Ironically enough, you can't without a dedicated routine and focus. Suppose you just start running, at no specific pace and with no goals set for distance or heart rate. Two weeks later, you decide to switch over to swimming. So you swim for a couple of months and then switch to aerobics. You have been dedicated to a cardio part of your workout, yet you realize you do not notice any significant changes (in other words, improvements) to your body fat level or physique. Without a fitness plan setting out your objectives and the specifics such as heart rate, duration, speed, distance, time, and intensity, you are truly spinning your wheels and not maximizing the cardio portion of your workout. Moreover, you're completely missing out on complementary fitness components, such as weight training.

THE VALUE OF CROSS-TRAINING

Mutual funds and fixed income products are two investment alternatives that offer diversity to the holdings in your portfolio. They offer a cross-training component to your investments. Perhaps the cash and equity components of your portfolio are adequately balanced to offer you the necessary liquidity (cash) and growth (stocks) that an investor like you needs. But if you put money only into stocks, leaving the remainder of your disposable income in a completely liquid state, you are limiting the potential performance of your assets.

In the fitness routine you develop, there is an emphasis on achieving your fitness goals through a mix of varied exercises and diet, ideally using efficiently the time that you dedicate to daily physical activity. Similarly, with your investment portfolio you need to emphasize achieving your goals through investment products that offer a variety of risk, return, and performance. Should you choose to restrict your investment activity to putting your money only into resource stocks, you should know that you may well obliterate all your hard-earned money if that particular sector turns sour. Diversification ensures that your assets will grow and that your financial goals, both short and long term, will be achieved. You need to be confident in your asset allocation and investment decisions. Putting all of your eggs into one basket (even if your hairdresser swears a stock tip is a sure thing!) is a recipe for disaster.

Mutual funds offer you the opportunity to hold in your portfolio a variety of holdings by becoming a unit holder in the fund. You can enjoy the security of having a professional investment manager choose the stocks that are held within that mutual fund, or bond fund, for that matter. The mutual fund company charges a management expense ratio (MER) for this service, and your financial consultant charges commission as payment for his or her service in finding the fund most suited to you.

Similarly, fixed income products spread out the risk associated with market investing, as there is generally more security associated with investing in bonds. The higher the rating assigned to a fixed income product, the higher the level of safety.

Cross-training introduces fresh elements of exercise into your workout routine, reduces the risk of injury associated with overuse of specific muscle groups, and increases the likelihood of successfully achieving your goals. Learning new components of a workout also increases your knowledge of the workings of your body and redefines your capabilities and physical limitations. Cross-training your portfolio holdings increases the performance potential, reduces risk, and furthers your working knowledge of the investment world.

MUTUAL FUNDS: PERFECT FOR CROSS-TRAINING

Generally speaking, mutual funds are to the stock market what cross-training is to your cardio workout. Most investors purchase mutual funds without fully comprehending what they are participating in. What is a mutual fund and why is it a cross-training vehicle for strengthening your investment portfolio?

A mutual fund is a pool of money that goes collectively towards purchasing stocks. The fund company sets up a fund that offers a specific style and area of investment — for example, a fund based on the top performers of the TSE 300 and S&P 500 (Toronto Stock Exchange's top 300 stocks and the New York Stock Exchange's top 500 stocks (listed by Standard & Poor)). The average investor does not have enough in her assets to go out and purchase these individual stocks. So a mutual fund is created to enable beginning and smaller portfolio investors to increase the potential performance of their money and dilute their risk by holding a variety of stocks rather than the one or two they would be able to afford on their own. The mutual fund manager takes the pooled money and uses it to purchase the stocks. The mutual fund now has a portfolio made up of these core holdings. The individual investor who could not own these stocks in her own portfolio can now hold units of this fund that represent a small portion of the mutual fund's actual stock portfolio.

This is how an investor can cross-train. Suppose you have just begun your investment portfolio and can only afford to contribute $100 per month. If you attempt to acquire your own holdings, your monetary allotment allows you to purchase only a very small portion of each stock; with $100 per month, it will be a long time before you can acquire a similar portfolio to that held by a mutual fund company.

The beauty of a mutual fund is that if you are a beginner to investing — and the size of your assets is limited — you automatically increase your diversification. When you buy stock, you usually buy a board lot (100 shares of a particular company), which can amount to a considerable sum of money. The price of buying stock is the market price times the number of shares wanted. Although usually the investor is required to buy a board lot, occasionally you can purchase a broken lot (less than 100 shares). But if you only have a few hundred dollars to invest on a monthly basis, a mutual fund investment is ideal. With an automatic payment plan, you can invest in a mutual fund that holds on average 30 to 100 companies in its portfolio. Instead of waiting for the day you can purchase shares of all 30 to 100 companies and be a shareholder, you can invest in the mutual fund and be a unit holder.

Finding the Right Fit

Choosing which mutual fund is right for you is similar to choosing your stock selection and asset allocation. More often than not the investor over-diversifies, over-pays annual fees and management fees (MERs), and falls into a pattern of investing based on last year's performance. This is not to say that mutual funds have no redeeming qualities, but that the merits need to be highlighted much more clearly to investors so they can avoid the pitfalls.

The best way to avoid these pitfalls is to educate yourself. You need to be able to compare the existing mutual funds out there. (A great Web site I have found quite useful is called the Globe Fund Web site, provided by the *Globe and Mail.*) You need to understand what your investment goals are, the level of risk you are comfortable with, and the management style that best suits you. Just as with all the other investment products, you should always keep your investment strategy in mind. In your physical workout too, you should always have a strategy. Know which body part you are working on, and which area you are resting. To lose sight of your workout structure is to risk injury. But injury within your financial world takes a lot longer to heal than a pulled muscle!

The two leading mutual fund strategies are growth and value. Growth funds are associated with large cap companies that are the blue chip industry leaders; the fund manager focuses on proven performance and consistent earnings. Value funds are poised to find the next "big thing" before its share price reflects its new-found status and ideally to invest when the company's stock is undervalued — that is, the manager attempts to buy really, really low and sell high.

Currently there are more mutual funds available than there are stocks. This fact highlights the importance of selecting the proper fund for you, and not necessarily following the herd. With so many mutual funds to choose from, the likelihood of choosing a poor performer is quite high. This probably doesn't seem exactly tragic, until you realize how much that poor choice will cost in your investment dollars. Most independent investors listen to the media trumpeting the mutual fund darling of the year before. Chick-A-Boom Chicks will not be rear-view mirror investors (and not because we are using it to put on lipstick!). The proper way to choose an appropriate mutual fund is through diligent research into the fund's holdings, manager, and past performance averages.

Software packages are available that provide a thorough breakdown of the top 15 holdings within a mutual fund, the percentage each company represents, and a multitude of comparison and performance graphs that will outline the fund. (One example of this is Pal Trak.) A great information source regarding mutual funds is in the books that review all of those currently available, such as *Chand's World of Mutual Funds* by Ranga Chand. Always keep in mind that past performance does not guarantee future results. If you are currently invested in a poor performer but you truly believe in both the mutual fund's portfolio make-up and the manager's investment philosophy, do not abandon ship. Investing in a mutual fund is not a recipe for overnight success. Never try to time the market, even in mutual funds. If you like the potential that this mutual fund appears to offer you, dedicate some time to the investment, and see if it can turn around. Always take a few minutes to contact your financial adviser to get a professional opinion on the holding and its potential performance. Advisers have access to more in-depth industry analysis than you do.

GETTING OUT ONTO THE FLOOR

Although mutual funds are a great way to attain immediate diversification while your asset size is limited, I always encourage individual investors to get into the market and participate in the buying and selling of individual stocks as soon as possible. The reason behind this is that the best way to appreciate market activity is to watch a company in which you are a shareholder have its stock price go up and down. Unit prices of mutual funds are listed in the daily newspapers as well, but the movements are normally quite fractional. To truly appreciate the action of the market, you need to buy, hold, and sell stocks. It's the same when you truly need to hit a cardio high — a pleasant walk is not going to stimulate the endorphins you so eagerly crave. A stock purchase would be analogous to a high-impact aerobics class, whereas a mutual fund purchase would be comparable to the pleasant walk. Both investment products represent participation within the equity sector, just as both forms of exercise help to achieve fitness goals.

This is an ideal time to once again discuss risk tolerance, in relation to the individual investor. When selecting an appropriate workout routine to whip your bod into shape, professional personal trainers are available to guide you from beginner status workouts up to the more advanced levels. You shouldn't attempt to hit a certain heart rate zone if you don't know what is ideal for you or if a certain rate is considered hazardous to your health. When you invest, you should always be comfortable with the amount of risk associated with the investments you have chosen. If you cannot afford to lose any of the money you have invested, you should choose a product that guarantees your principal, such as a government savings bond. But if you can handle a bit of risk and invest in a product that does not provide a safety net of 100% protection, you can get involved in a larger variety of investments.

FIXED AND FIRM

"If I lift heavy weights, I am going to bulk up like a guy — as a curvaceous chic, this is highly unappealing." Wrong!

"If I put my money into a bond that doesn't mature until 10 years from now, I am going to miss out on stock market opportunities and growth potentials." Wrong again!

Weights increase your muscle tone and definition. It is not the amount of weight you lift that delivers the results as much as it is the actual routine, style, and control of movement. You need to develop a program that includes all the major and minor muscle groups and works these muscles in a controlled and challenging manner. Weight training enables your body to be strong enough to perform successfully in the cardio, stretching, and conditioning portions of your workout. It also delivers the power you need for effective day-to-day living. Weight lifting should rotate the muscle groups so that each area worked has a full 24 hours' rest before it is worked again, because weight lifting actually causes slight tears in the muscle tissue, which needs a full day to recover. The healing process results in stronger muscle tissue, so your weight routine produces improved strength and tonality.

Fixed income is a necessary part of your investment portfolio. Just as weight training works in conjunction with the cardio component of your workout, fixed income complements the equity portion of your portfolio. It represents the conservative section of your investments, and it enhances the balance of your portfolio. If all you have in your portfolio is fixed income products, you will achieve only a limited return. If all you do during your workout is lift weights, your results will reflect that. You will not be in a strong cardiovascular condition, nor will your elasticity or flexibility be at peak.

However, if you assign a certain percentage of your portfolio to the asset allocation of fixed income, your overall investments will reflect proper diversification. Balance: it ensures that an investor can sleep well at night and not be in a constant state of panic about market performance or suffer interest rate revulsion. Dividing your assets into equity, cash, and fixed income reflects a strategy of conservatism and growth. This strategy, along with the time element, is a recipe for successful investing. You are in the stock market so you can enjoy the potential advances offered by it. At the same time, you have placed some of your assets into fixed income to participate in a more staid rate of growth, albeit guaranteed. The cash within your portfolio is for opportunities and/or just plain liquidity.

Introducing weight training into your fitness regime is a slow process that emphasizes technique and conditioning. You start off with light weights and focus on training your muscles to control movement and breathing. Only when you have mastered the basics will you be ready to increase the weight. Developing a solid weight program is an extremely slow process with much emphasis on education and good conditioning. You'll spend long arduous hours focusing on body positioning, muscle control, breathing, posture, and control. The weight lifted is far less important than your technique. If you fail to develop the proper technique, you will experience injuries and accidents, guaranteed. Fixed income investments are similar to developing a weight-lifting regimen, but here the emphasis is on choosing high-yielding products with low risk and a high-grade rating, so your focus should not be on duration.

The life of the fixed income product should not be your main concern. Because there is a fairly liquid secondary market available, an investor can choose to sell off a bond; there are usually buyers who are more than happy to complete the transaction equation. Check with a financial consultant about liquidity and the yield curve before jumping into the fixed income market. Most fixed income products can be assigned to one of two schools: corporate or government issues.

Investors should recognize the importance of holding fixed income products as a solid component within a portfolio. Whether you invest in stocks or mutual funds, you will experience market volatility at some time. The fixed income component of your portfolio provides a solid base to your investments, and acts as a great form of advanced savings. The bonds deliver a rate of return that is usually higher than the prime rate so that your money's rate of growth is relatively appealing. Fixed income investing is not viewed by many people as a particularly sexy investment product, but there is something to be said for guaranteeing the safety of your money and knowing in advance what the rate of return is going to be.

Let's say you purchase a GMAC (corporate bond from General Motors) for $10,000 earning 6.5% interest, and its maturity date is February 12, 2009. Does this mean you have to hold this product until the year 2009? Absolutely not! As previously mentioned, you could take advantage of the secondary market and sell the GMAC a week from this Tuesday if you chose to. In the meantime, your money would be earning its 6.5% interest — do you know what your savings account at the bank is earning? Probably less than 2%.

Lifting weights is a fantastic means of defining your body shape, and the changes are impressive if you are dedicated to a routine and diet. Keep in mind that you will not even notice any of these changes for the first three to four months of a new program. This may seem like a fairly large drawback, but instant changes in the body are never a good thing. Crash diets, steroid use, and excessive exercise all represent irresponsible treatment of your body and should never be a route you follow. The same precautions should be taken with your investments. If it seems too good to be true, it probably is. There is no such thing as a get-rich-quick investment plan, and as a wise and worldly Chick, I would love to witness your reaction to some slimy broker who tried to sell you on one of these schemes!

Your Fixed Income Options

The products available in the fixed income world range from corporate bonds, government bonds, preferred shares, mutual funds that are fixed-income focused, strip bonds, GICs, and retirement savings bonds. Corporate bonds usually offer a higher rate, but the rating of the bond is usually a lower grade than that associated with a government bond. Bonds are offered by federal, provincial, and municipal governments. The grade rating on government bonds is often a very interesting reflection on the political and socio-economic state of each country, province, or city. The rates are usually lower on government bonds. The reasoning behind this is that there is less likelihood of a country, province, or municipality going bankrupt than a corporation, therefore less risk is associated with the product. When you choose the fixed income portion of your portfolio, be sure to take into account all factors such as quality and historical performance. Don't just focus on the rate of return. Ideally, you will be able to locate a product that offers stability, top quality, *and* a decent rate of return on your investment.

Preferred shares are interesting investment instruments that combine the stock market risk and excitement with fixed income security. Preferred shares offer dividend yields while at the same time participating in the equity growth. Considerably higher risk is associated with preferred shares compared to government bonds, but because of the dividends they are considered fixed income instruments.

Some mutual funds focus strictly on fixed income instruments, commonly referred to as bond funds. These funds combine a bond manager's proven track record and experience with a basket of different bonds offering a variety of rates of return. This is a great product, especially when the manager has excellent skills. Locating a good fixed income instrument is not an easy task, and if there is a fund available that provides you with what you want, paying for the service is sometimes the best option. Not only do you receive the benefit of a professional manager and a variety of fixed income instruments offering varied rates of return, but you also have guaranteed liquidity.

Suppose the bond market takes a nosedive and the paper value of bonds is obliterated. You and every other fixed income investor are going to be attempting to sell your bonds on the secondary market. The only problem is one of simple supply and demand economics: too much supply and no demand equal valueless bonds nobody is prepared to buy from you! However, if you are a bond fund unit holder and the same nosedive occurs in the bond market, you can simply redeem your units with a phone call to your adviser; usually by the end of that business day, you are in a liquid position (some funds vary on redemption availability, so always check with your adviser or read through the prospectus). The *Chick-A-Boom* glossary provides you with a working definition of these fixed income products; if you have further questions about fixed income instruments, get on the Internet or engage a financial consultant.

Fixed income instruments are comparable to your muscular system in that they support your infrastructure. The more strongly you develop your muscles, the more protected from injury your skeleton is. Similarly, if your portfolio is diversified to include fixed income products, the market volatility will have less of an impact on your financial status.

There is one fantastic bonus associated with weight lifting, and I have been saving it for now. Weight lifting increases your metabolism rate while reducing your body fat. Think about it! When you increase the variety of your exercise regime, you increase your enjoyment of exercise. When you expand your exercise regime to include weights, you reduce your body fat, and increase your muscular definition. When your exercise regime includes weights, your metabolism rate increases. Life is good! The fabulous merits of weights are mirrored in fixed income instruments. Liquidity, higher rates of return, and a conservative manner increase your sense of financial security while simultaneously enabling you to enjoy the participation of the equity market. Life is good!

When you walk into an aerobics studio for the first time, you may be slightly intimidated by the other members, the regulars who attend religiously and are fanatical about their space and their positioning in front of the mirror and the instructor. They know the music from the first beat and can go through the class without cueing from the instructor. They seem to be the ones with a hint of a smirk when new people make mistakes during class, and they are usually the ones who make that annoying "whooping" noise, like they're in a disco from the eighties! These aerobics studio regulars provide us with a strong message we should heed: Overconfidence and a cocky attitude almost always deliver a false sense of security, an attitude of false expertise.

Keep an open mind, and be eager to continue the learning process. Whether you are investing in individual stocks, mutual funds, fixed income products, or any combination thereof, always make the effort to learn as much as you can. Continue to learn about what it is that you own, what it is currently doing in the market, what its future endeavours are expected to be, and how its performance relates to that of its competitors. In the investment world, it is an absolute recipe for disaster to sit back and assume that what you have invested in today can be left alone and be worth what you expect tomorrow. A classic example is the commodity of gold. Had you asked your grandparents what you should invest in when you were 10 years old, their answer could almost be guaranteed to be gold. Today the answer is definitely something else. Similarly, there were a whole ton of leg warmers and matching head bands in the fitness world 10 years ago. Need I say more?

5

ABDOMINALS

Retirement Planning Takes a Strong Stomach

A bdominals are called "abominables" for a reason — everyone hates that particular part of their workout, yet everyone loves the results, namely the 6-pack stomach. The same thing can be said of planning for your retirement. It is an utter drag having to prepare for your *golden* years during your *now* years. Yet it is imperative to get these preparations under way as early as possible — or else develop a liking for shopping carts and Tender Vittles! Scare tactics are neither my message nor my medium of choice, but unfortunately the reality is much more frightening than my humour.

Women live longer and earn less. Simple but true. Despite the social advances in education and careers, women still have barriers to cross in order to increase their financial security and status. Women often take time off to be care givers, whether for their children or for their parents. With the baby boomers entering the retirement years, the responsibilities of their children will greatly increase. If you are wondering whether the boomers' shift will in any way affect you and your life, ask yourself one easy question: What have the boomers ever done quietly? As discussed earlier, the greatest shift of wealth ever from one generation to another is about to occur between the boomers and their children. The large population shift into retirement will also greatly reduce the government pension funds available, so if you were planning on retiring off the government's money stash, it may be time to reassess your retirement plan.

PLANNING FOR RETIREMENT

Early in 1999, an article in the *Globe and Mail* stated that 10% of Canadians have quite an interesting financial plan for financing their retirement: winning the lottery! Well, yeah, wouldn't we all like to have those lucky numbers smiling up at us from a little piece of paper? Unfortunately, there is a better chance of the federal government finding a cash-stuffed vault in the basement of an old Parliament building and putting it all towards doubling the CPP allowance for each Canadian. Sorry to rain on the fantasy parade, but the only sure-fire path to a secure retirement is participation in an RRSP.

Without strong abdominal muscles, your lower back has no support. Without adequate planning for your retirement, your senior years will have no financial support. The truly amazing feature of a registered plan is that the government works with you and rewards you for placing money in a registered retirement account. There is one point to remember about making the most of the government's generosity — maximize your participation now, before the generosity changes.

The money you put into your RRSP is tax-sheltered. That means you do not have to acknowledge (that is, pay) for the capital gains and income that result from the growth of your funds until you are 69 years old, when you expect to be in a lower tax bracket and in retirement. To make the idea even more attractive, you receive immediate benefits from contributing to an RRSP in the form of a tax credit. You get an immediate income tax deduction for the year contributions are made. This means you pay less tax in the year of contribution. Think of this as maintaining a sleek, flat stomach with fewer crunches than it initially took to get there. You've acknowledged the problem of your flabby stomach and have started an abdominal routine. The initial step is always the most difficult, but once you see the results, you are encouraged and your initiative and drive to succeed are only increased!

The same thing happens when you start your RRSP contributions. At first you think there is no way that this measly little amount of money is ever going to amount to anything that will support the lifestyle you have imagined for your retirement years. But through the power of compounding interest and a strong portfolio performance, RRSPs are the best way to achieve your retirement goals.

Strong abdominal muscles are necessary for lower-back support and for respiratory and digestive functions. The aesthetic justification of developing your abdominal region comes in a 6-pack! In comparison to the cardio, the abdominal portion of your workout involves less time. Despite the savings in time, the excuses that abound to avoid exercising the abs are seemingly limitless, not to mention entertaining. The same is true about contributing to and developing your retirement savings. Excuses, avoidance, and procrastination — and why not? After all, retirement planning is for older people, right? Wrong! The time to start planning and saving for your retirement is yesterday. The main benefit of starting early is compound interest and the growth it can contribute to your RRSP. Compound interest is paid on interest earned as well as on the principal, and in an RRSP the compounding interest is tax-sheltered.

The following example highlights the most significant benefit offered by compounding interest through a comparison of two clients. The first client is a clever young person who begins investing $2,500 annually for a 10-year period only during her 20s and then leaves her RRSP account alone. The second client is a little slower off the mark in beginning to invest in her retirement plan, and contributes $2,500 annually from the age of 30 for 35 years until she turns 65. Here comes the truly amazing part of this example: guess who had a larger RRSP at retirement? The smart young client, *who invested $65,000 less*, ended up, through the miracle of compounding interest, with almost $300,000 *more* when she reached the age of 65:

	THIRTY-SOMETHING CLIENT	SMART YOUNG CLIENT
Contribution Total	$ 90,000	$ 25,000
RRSP Value	$ 643,440	$ 921,217

The lesson is both concise and precise: start contributing to your RRSP as soon as possible. To procrastinate any longer is to risk the lifestyle you want to have during your retirement. Financial self-sufficiency is the best goal for women to set when thinking about retirement savings. The actual amount that each individual requires for retirement is a calculation that each of us needs to make, with the assistance of a financial plan, a clear understanding of risk tolerance, and a financial consultant with whom you have chosen to work to achieve your goals.

Whether you are in your 20s and have already started contributing to your RRSP, getting well ahead in your retirement planning, or in your late 40s and now consider it a good time to open an RRSP, you should take a moment and congratulate yourself! As long as you recognize the need for some money to be available to you during your senior years, you are on the right track and success is on its way. There is no such thing as "too late" when it comes to opening an RRSP and starting contributions for your retirement — unless of course you have already retired! Here's a rule of thumb for all Chick-a-Boom investors: It is never too late to begin investing in yourself. The same holds true for exercise: It is never too late to invest in your own health and physical well-being!

While it is never too late to begin investing in yourself and your retirement years, the value of starting off at a young age cannot be overstated. Consider the chart on pages 102–3, which outlines RRSP contributions made by Catherine between the ages of 30 and 65 years of age, when she managed to maximize her contributions, putting $13,500 — the maximum amount allowed by the government — into her RRSP each year. (Some of her contributions in the earlier years were made with a bank loan taken out specifically for RRSP contributions.) The numbers speak for themselves — take your inspiration from them.

Now as impressive as Catherine's portfolio may seem, she will in fact need to increase the performance of her investment portfolio or else maximize her savings outside the RRSP account in order to have enough money to fund her retirement years. Fortunately, she has developed a solid relationship with her financial adviser and her RRSP is not the only financial vehicle she has to fund her retirement. She realized

CATHERINE'S ANNUAL MAXIMIZED RRSP CONTRIBUTIONS
(ASSUMING A 10% RETURN ON HER PORTFOLIO)

AGE	CUMULATIVE RRSP CONTRIBUTIONS	RRSP VALUE
30	$13,500	$14,850
31	27,000	29,700
32	40,500	44,550
33	54,000	59,400
34	67,500	74,250
35	81,000	89,100
36	94,500	103,950
37	108,000	118,800
38	121,500	133,650
39	135,000	148,500
40	148,500	163,350
41	162,000	178,200
42	175,500	193,050
43	189,000	207,900
44	202,500	222,750
45	216,000	237,600
46	229,500	252,450
47	243,000	267,300
48	256,500	282,150
49	270,000	297,000
50	283,500	311,850
51	297,000	326,700
52	310,500	341,550
53	324,000	356,400
54	337,500	371,250
55	351,000	386,100
56	364,500	400,950
57	378,000	415,800

CATHERINE'S ANNUAL MAXIMIZED RRSP CONTRIBUTIONS
(ASSUMING A 10% RETURN ON HER PORTFOLIO) CONT'D

AGE	CUMULATIVE RRSP CONTRIBUTIONS	RRSP VALUE
58	391,500	430,650
59	405,000	445,500
60	418,500	460,350
61	432,000	475,200
62	445,500	490,050
63	459,000	504,900
64	472,500	519,750
65	486,000	534,600

early on, by identifying her short- and long-term goals, and communicating them to her financial adviser, that the $534,600 she would end up with at age 65, assuming maximum yearly contributions and a 10% interest rate, would represent only half of what she would need to lead the kind of retirement lifestyle she desires.

Similarly, if you are in your late 50s and are considering opening an RRSP account in order to take advantage of its the tax-sheltering abilities during the last 10 years you will be working, the funds might accrue as Sue's did.

Sue's chart, on the next page, emphasizes the point that it is truly never too late to initiate your retirement savings. If you have concerns about your financial fitness in the future, perhaps starting your retirement financial planning will alleviate some of your worry and concerns. Play with some numbers, either on your own spreadsheet or with the assistance of your financial adviser. Once you have an idea of what it will take to get you to the financial point you wish to reach, your fear of the unknown will be removed.

SUE'S $10,000 ANNUAL RRSP CONTRIBUTIONS
(ASSUMING A 15% RETURN ON HER PORTFOLIO)

AGE	CUMULATIVE RRSP CONTRIBUTIONS	RRSP VALUE
55	10,000	11,500
56	20,000	23,000
57	30,000	34,500
58	40,000	46,000
59	50,000	57,500
60	60,000	69,000
61	70,000	80,500
62	80,000	92,000
63	90,000	103,500
64	100,000	115,000
65	110,000	126,500

When you think about your fitness level and body fat measurement, you recognize the need to join a gym, start exercising, and improve your eating habits. But let's be reasonable! Someone who is not exactly thrilled with the way their body looks is not going to hit the gym in a cute little Lycra job. In reality, when we feel intimidated by our less than ideal state, initiating change is an extremely difficult endeavour. However, once the first step is made, change is right around the corner. Acknowledging fear of the situation is the first step to achieving your goals. So make an appointment to tour a health club and ask questions about the training programs. Afterwards, make an appointment with a financial adviser and ask questions about your financial fitness. These meetings are complimentary and what you get out of them is immeasurable!

Crunching your midriff into a state of definition is a long

road that seems seldom to offer hints of improvement or encouragement. Nobody points out that your abdominal muscles will not miraculously pop through the fatty tissue that has kept you more than warm for the last few seasons! Nobody tells you that joining that health club in January means that physical results will begin to show on your inside and outside around March or April if you maintain a strong dedication to your routine. Both physical and financial fitness demand dedication, and you need patience and faith: patience in attaining your goals, and faith in yourself and your plan. The same observation can be made about your RRSP account. You will probably not even notice the initial growth or contributions, and will probably question the actual value of such seemingly small steps. But just refer back to that graph and see how quickly growth occurred for both clients.

The Truth about RRSPs

You may believe that a simple sit-up is all you need to develop your stomach — after all, your stomach is just one ball of muscle, right? Nope! When you work your abdominals, you may not realize it but there are four muscle groups that you are working: upper, transverse, obliques, lower. And if you stopped yanking on your neck muscles and relying on that rocking momentum for just a minute, you could develop a conditioning routine that would provide you with results. Just focusing on your muscle groups and controlling the movement so that it is precise and concise will produce gratifying results. The assumption that your abdominals are just one muscle is very similar to the assumption that an RRSP is a product unto itself

— it is not a product, it is a type of investment account.

Attention, Chicks! Repeat after me: "I cannot go out and buy RRSPs."

I am quite certain that a few of you have previously understood that you bought RRSPs through your bank, and I am here to let you know that this is just not the case. You cannot go out and "buy an RRSP"; you can, however, open an RRSP account and start to contribute towards financial security in your retirement years. There is a great misconception in the general public that an RRSP is an entity unto itself, which has no flexibility in its composition. This is quite simply not true. An RRSP account offers exactly the same capabilities and can hold the same investment instruments as an investment account. The only differences are that the RRSP account is tax-sheltered until retirement and that you must limit your foreign content to 20% of your total portfolio value. Otherwise, the account is able to hold cash, stocks and equities, and fixed income instruments and you are able to contribute annually and make investment transactions at any time so as to increase the performance of your holdings.

An RRSP is like your locker in the health club change room. When you join a health club, you are assigned a locker. It is an empty metal box that protects your valuables while you work out. You can choose what belongings should be inside, based upon your needs. You can place your jewellery, your wallet, your clothing, and some toiletries into this locker. You can choose to keep a full supply of shampoo, conditioner, and all of your hair care products inside so that you have all the products you normally use at home. Similarly, you could choose to keep only a skeleton of supplies. It is completely up to you what is kept inside your locker. No one has access to it because of the lock, and your belongings are safe.

Your RRSP is quite similar in structure. It is not a single entity unto itself, but rather a holding tank for a multitude of investment products. When you open an RRSP account, it is a bubble ready to be filled up. You can put any mixture of mutual funds, stocks, bonds, and cash into it, and you can mould it with diversification just as in any other investment account. The only difference with this account is the wonderfully delicious RRSP trait of being tax-sheltered! Canada offers few tax breaks, so all Canadians should take full advantage of tax-sheltered RRSP money until retirement. Understanding how these rules and regulations work is really quite simple, when you focus on the basics.

The maximum amount you can contribute to your RRSP on a yearly basis is 18% of your earned income, up to a maximum of $13,500. Don't panic if you have not contributed to your RRSP before — there is still hope. A neat feature called carry forward is a beneficial instrument set up to help investors play catch-up. You are permitted to go all the way back to your 1991 contribution and carry forward any unused RRSP contribution values. To determine your personal contribution room, take a look at your annual tax return; in the package you will find Revenue Canada's Notice of Assessment. The assessment shows you your allowable RRSP contribution room, including any amount that may be left over. Keeping in mind that only 60% of Canadians have set up RRSP accounts and less than 40% of those who have RRSPs maximize their contributions, I am willing to bet that a few of you have some room available.

There is another break offered by the government, and that is the over-contribution limit. This rule stipulates that you are allowed a lifetime amount of up to $2,000 of over-contributions in your RRSP.

Speaking of lifetime, the time frame available for contributing to your RRSP is up to December 31 of the year you reach the age of 69. After that, you must roll over the account into a Registered Retirement Income Fund (RRIF), which is a fund from which you make withdrawals in accordance with tax and Revenue Canada regulations, thus finally being able to access the money from your RRSP.

Your RRSP account also offers a few well-hidden treats involving your first home. You can transfer $20,000 from your RRSP to the mortgage of your first home. The money must be paid back in 15 years, and you must realize the risk involved: yes, you receive an interest-free loan, but the risk is in forgoing the potential growth of your RRSP during the years the money is otherwise engaged. When deciding whether to exercise this RRSP option, speak to your financial adviser to compare the potential outcomes.

The cost of post-secondary education can also be addressed through your RRSP and involves the government giving you money. No, that is not a misprint. An RESP is an investment instrument that allows an annual contribution of $4,000 up to a lifetime limit of $42,000 per beneficiary, and the federal government tops up your contribution by 20% each year. So, if you contribute $2,000 towards your child's university education, the government will add $400, making your total contribution for the year $2,400. Not a bad deal! There is some flexibility with this RESP money as you can absorb it into your own RRSP if the child does not go on to a post-secondary institution. At that time, you can use the money for your own tuition purposes should you decide to take some university or college courses. There are some particulars regarding this feature, so check with your financial consultant regarding limits.

Always contribute to your RRSP early in the year so as to increase its value. Through compounding interest, the value of the RRSP will be much greater if you put your money in during March instead of waiting until the following January. Most Canadians believe that RRSP season is January and February because the media deliver this message. What the savvy Chick-A-Boom investor will now understand is that she should invest in her RRSP at the beginning of each year, and if she cannot do so because of financial restrictions, at the very least she should contribute on a monthly basis to increase her portfolio's investment potential value.

Although the existing RRSP system with its various characteristics is a fabulous opportunity for individual investors, ideally you will want to maximize your contributions going forward. Keep in mind that it is impossible to predict changes to the RRSP rules in future governmental budgets.

RRSPs and Foreign Content

Maximizing foreign exposure is vital. You are permitted to invest 20% of your RRSP's value in foreign holdings. This means you can buy investment products from anywhere else in the world, the U.S., Europe, Asia, anywhere but Canada. The skill needed for foreign investing can be achieved in the same way as any other type of skill — through education. Reading and research always help, as does meeting with your financial adviser and discussing your international interests. You should also study the investment patterns evolving on the international scene.

Make every attempt to reach a 20% foreign equity content so you do not limit the potential performance of your money. Canada represents only 3% of the international market, yet

80% of your RRSP must be Canadian content. A majority of investors do not take advantage of the 20% window, and that is a real shame.

Imagine if you only ever walked on a treadmill for your workout regime and never ventured into any other fitness activities. Boring! You'd achieve limited results for all your hard work. If you only walked on the treadmill and never thought to exercise your midriff region, your flabby abs would be an advertisement for your poor training routine, and your swimsuit selection would be quite limited. If a large portion of your body is never challenged, a large portion of your body will *show* that it has never been challenged! However, if your workout includes a day on the treadmill, another day working with weights, and another doing aerobics, the results and conditioning of your body will be maximized.

Limited performance delivers limited results. The foreign market offers a buffer zone to the domestic markets and economies. When you're investing for your retirement, a buffer zone is a great thing to have. As mentioned in Chapter 4, foreign markets do not always reflect domestic market conditions. Suppose the North American economy suddenly tanked, our dollar dropped in value (yes, even further than today's value!), and your RRSP's value went south with the dollar. You had, however, decided to maximize your foreign content, so had 20% of your portfolio divided among investments in Asia, Europe, and the United States. These investments continued to thrive as a result of the foreign markets having banner bull runs, so your RRSP losses were lessened.

One final note on the 20% foreign exposure rule: Always keep a close eye on your foreign content as you will be taxed by the federal government on any extra foreign holdings.

Retirement Fitness

Your abdominals are the support for your torso, your respiratory system, your lower back, and your digestive organs. You need to ensure their development and strength in order to maximize your everyday performance and health. Your RRSP is the support for your retirement; without proper development, your golden years may be spent under arches asking, "Do you want fries with that?" Take a few minutes to meet with a financial consultant to identify your long-term goals, and initiate an investment plan to reflect these goals. Think about what it is you will be doing in retirement — what the lifestyle you plan to lead will involve. The answers you provide will directly influence just how aggressive an investor you need to be *now* in your working years.

The worst part about retirement planning is that the numbers can be extremely intimidating, no matter how ample your salary appears to be today. It is estimated that the individual Canadian citizen will need at least $1 million to fund his or her retirement. This estimate is actually conservative. Will you want to travel the world or perhaps purchase a retirement home in the south? Will you be healthy, or should you plan ahead to include medical expenditures and nursing home costs, just in case? Where will you live, and how important is the quality of your surroundings and your quality of life? Will it be important that you leave assets to your estate? How big is your family? Will all of your surviving relations receive a piece of your estate?

The answers to all these questions will help provide you with a template for your financial plan for retirement. I highly advise you to consult not only with your financial adviser but also with an accountant and a lawyer about estate and tax issues. This trio of professionals can assist you with calculations and estimations regarding your retirement financial projections to ensure that you achieve your dreams.

Retirement planning is not nearly as intimidating a process as most people assume; in fact, it is similar to trying on a bathing suit in January. At the time, the prospect seems almost impossible and yet somehow the calendar year moves aggressively towards July and then presto, you are in a bathing suit, your abs are nicely developed, and the only stress in your life is what level of sun protection you need!

Abdominal development is a slow process that requires your dedication and unfaltering long-range vision. The long-term benefits will surely outlast the initial frustration of slow-to-achieve results. The best quality of a well-developed abdominal region is that it becomes your strongest motivator for continuous exercise. Once the stomach area is developed and toned, you will do pretty much anything to maintain those cut muscles. The same goes for your retirement savings, although it may seem quite impossible that these initial, paltry monthly contributions may someday fund your golden years. But once asset growth begins, your appetite as an investor will increase dramatically. The power of compound interest is such that minimum dollar contributions will suddenly become the buying leverage for multiple portfolio holdings.

6

COOL-DOWN

Cool Your Risk Aversion with Comprehensive Confidence

You walk into the health club for the very first time and listen to the "gym-speak"; quite frankly they might as well be speaking Swahili. Bench press? Why wouldn't you use weights and leave the furniture alone? Squats, abs, cardio, reps — then you enter the aerobics studio and it is really game over. Grapevine, v-step, basic alternate, tae-bo, hip-hop, boxercise . . . How exactly does everyone know what to do and when?

Similarly, when you enter the world of investing, the complex terminology can leave you feeling helpless at first. There seems to be a logical process at work here, but what is it? How do some people seem to find the perfect time to move? Initially, the terminology and concepts may seem foreign to the inexperienced investor. But just as with a fitness routine, you must start off with the basics before graduating to the advanced levels. You aspire to improve your physical fitness to increase your quality of life, and you should be investing in the same spirit.

Developing a new exercise routine can be intimidating because although you know what your goals are (e.g., to lose 10 pounds, develop muscle where there is currently fat, get rid of that cottage cheese at the back of your legs, and develop a washboard stomach), you aren't quite sure how to get there. That is when you bring in a personal trainer, to ensure you are avoiding injury and maximizing your energy to achieve the goal. Once you have the initial basics mastered, your routine can be readjusted to increase the workout and the results to maintain growth.

The same process can be applied to investing — the basics need to be learned and then the advice of a professional can increase your understanding of how to invest and the performance of your money. As was previously touched upon, investing is an ongoing procedure that demands continuous research, even if that research is limited to keeping up on current events and keeping abreast of political, social, and economic trends that may have some impact on you, your financial goals, and your portfolio holdings.

The worst mistake you can make is to not initiate some sort of investment plan. You need to become well versed in the world of investing and financial planning. If you were over-weight and your diet consisted of a weekly assault on the main fast-food joints in town, do you not think that your family physician and your family and friends would express concern? Do you not think that exercise would be introduced into your daily life so as to reduce the likelihood of heart disease and help reduce your body fat and weight?

The same argument holds true for your financial future: You need to establish a financial routine and participate in investing in order to ensure the comfort of your retirement years, as well as your peace of mind and quality of life in the here and now. Exercise and fitness are imperative ingredients to a positive, healthy, energy-filled existence. Investing your hard-earned dollars to maximize the performance of those dollars is essential to a prosperous, independent, self-enhanced existence. In short, how can you not look after yourself? Be a Chick-A-Boom Chick and develop your own financial fitness.

GLOSSARY

The best way to learn more about investing, financial planning, and increasing the potential of your assets would be to enrol in the Canadian Securities Course. But as you already have way too much on your plate with your career, family, friends, and your absolutely unfaltering dedication to your physical and financial fitness routines, I have included this quick reference glossary to assist you in your ongoing education about financial fitness and the investment world. Another valuable source of financial fitness information is the Internet. There are numerous Web sites available to help answer your investing questions. All the major investment firms have their own Web sites, and these usually include glossaries, question and answer pages, access to their research, and direct links to financial advisers. Most major mutual fund firms also have Web sites available for you to visit. For general information, I strongly recommend using a search engine and simply typing in your area of interest.

Annual Report — An information piece that summarizes a company's operations and financial performance over the past business year. It must include audited financial statements that outline the business, its operation, income sources, profits, losses, and bottom line net worth.

Asset — Any possession with value (although a great wardrobe might not qualify for inclusion) that is owned by an individual.

Asset Allocation — The dynamic distribution of investment assets into various categories such as bonds, common stocks, real estate, etc. in response to assumptions regarding future economic and market conditions.

Back-End Redemption Charge — Also called a deferred sales charge (DSC). Some mutual funds have no front-end charges or load when they are acquired, but do levy back or rear-end charges (load) when the fund units are redeemed. This charge declines each year the units are held until it reaches zero. There is always a choice.

Balanced Funds — Mutual funds that combine safety, income, and capital appreciation. A portfolio of fixed income securities and a broad group of common stocks. The asset mix reduces the risk through diversification.

Benchmark — Any federal or provincial bond used by traders as a standard 5-, 10-, or 30-year issue. Usually benchmark issues are highly liquid bonds with a large quantity outstanding. A simpler definition: a standard against which something else is measured.

Bonds — Evidence of loans to corporations and governments made by investors in return for a fixed amount of interest. The borrowers promise to repay the loan by a certain date and to pay interest regularly to the investors in the interim.

Book Value — The difference between what a company owns and what it owes. The book value of a stock is the difference between what an individual investor paid for it and what its current market price is.

Canadian Investor Protection Fund (CIPF) — A fund set up by the stock exchanges and Investment Dealers Association to protect investors from losses resulting from the bankruptcy of a member firm.

Capital — Wealth in the form of money or property that is usually available for investment.

Capital Appreciation — An increase in the market value of money or property.

Cash — Short-term government obligations offering maximum liquidity and safety, e.g., Treasury Bills.

Closed-End Mutual Fund — Mutual funds that trade on a stock exchange like a stock. They are rarely written up or promoted by analysts and this can create value. Many, although not all, trade *below* their net asset value. The "net asset value" (NAV) is the current value of the investments in the fund's portfolio divided by the number of shares outstanding, a sort of net worth per share. But the market price of the shares can be higher or lower than the actual NAV depending on the forces of supply and demand in the market. Shares that can be bought at less than their NAV are said to be at a "discount."

This discount can, over the long term, lead to superior performance and acts as a defensive measure in times of market weakness. These funds are not subject to new money coming in or sudden redemptions like open-end funds, so managers can buy and sell based on their own discretion, and not on a sudden cash need by investors.

Common Stocks — Shares of ownership in a corporation — often referred to simply as "stock" — that are available to all investors.

Compounding — The longer and more you invest, the greater the potential return on your investment, as the return on your assets compounds over time. Interest is paid on the amount of interest already earned, as well as on principal. Compounding can occur daily, monthly, quarterly, or annually. It benefits the investor and saver but goes against the borrower.

Cyclical Stocks — Stocks that are closely linked to the economic and industrial conditions of a country, as is the stock's performance and value. Examples of cyclical stocks are oil and gas. In the winter months, the price of an oil or gas stock will usually be higher, and the colder and longer the winter, the better for the stock price.

Deferred Sales Charge (DSC) — See Back-End Redemption Charge.

Diversification — Spreading investment risk by buying different types of investment products in different sectors within different countries. This ensures that investment capital, and thus risk, is not concentrated in one area.

Dividend — An amount determined by a company's board of directors and paid out to holders of the company's common and/or preferred shares. A dividend may be paid in cash or in additional shares and is calculated on a per-share basis, usually quarterly. While dividends on common shares fluctuate with the profitability of the company, dividends on preferred shares are usually fixed.

Earnings Per Share — A company's profits divided by the number of shares outstanding (held by outside investors).

Equity — The ownership interest of common and preferred shareholders in a corporation. Used interchangeably with the term stock. Also refers to net worth.

Financial Plan — A plan that outlines your financial status and your financial goals both on a short- and long-term basis, and ideally provides suggestions to successfully achieve these goals. A financial plan should be reviewed on at least an annual basis.

Fixed Income Products — Investment instruments that guarantee a fixed rate of return over an agreed upon time frame. An example is a 5%, 10-year term government savings bond, with a triple A rating.

Front-End Load — An acquisition fee charged by many mutual funds, based on a percentage of total value of the units purchased. Generally, the percentage level of the fee decreases as the dollar amount of the transaction increases.

Income — Earnings, generally from interest or dividends, that are credited or paid to an investor.

Interest — The cost of using money. A borrower pays interest to a lender, usually a percentage of the loan amount. Keep in mind that it is much more pleasing to pay interest on a loan to increase your portfolio than it is to pay interest on credit cards.

Market Value — The current price of an asset, as indicated by the most recent price at which the asset was traded on the open market.

Mutual Fund — An investment product that pools investors' money to purchase a basket of stocks and securities on behalf of these investors. This mutual fund's resulting portfolio is owned by the collective independent investors, and as such they are unit holders of this mutual fund. The amount of money the individual investor puts into the mutual fund is reflected in the number of units held.

Net Asset Value (NAV) — The current value of the investments in a mutual fund's portfolio divided by the number of shares outstanding, a sort of net worth per share.

Portfolio — The stocks, bonds, and other assets owned by an investor or by a mutual fund.

Preferred Stock — A class of share capital that entitles owners to a fixed dividend ahead of the company's common shares, with a stated dollar value per share in the event of liquidation. Owners of preferred stock do not usually have voting rights unless a stated number of dividends have been withheld by the company.

Tax Deferred — Income that is not subject to taxation in the current year, but will be taxable at a future date when money is withdrawn from the sheltered account.

Total Return — The rate of return on an investment, including all dividends and interest, plus or minus any change in the value of the asset. Also, an investment strategy that seeks a combination of growth and income.

Treasury Bills — Short-term government debt issued in denominations ranging from $1,000 to $1 million. Treasury bills do not pay interest, but are sold at a discount and mature at par (100% of face value). The difference between the purchase price and par at maturity represents the lender's (purchaser's) income in lieu of interest. In Canada such gain is taxed as interest income in the purchaser's hands.

Yield — The return on an investment.